# ASSERTION OF GRACE

or,

A Defense of the Doctrine of Free Justification against the lawless, unjust and uncharitable imputation of Legalists & Pharisees, or the Favorites of Antichrist, who under a pretended zeal of the Law, do pervert, dispute and obscure the simplicity of the Faith of the Gospel.

Containing an Answer to that book entitled, The Rule of the Law under the Gospel, &c., which book set forth by Dr. Taylor is showed to be full of scandal and danger, as it was sent to the said Doctor a little before his death,

### By ROBERT TOWNE,

Minister of the Gospel.

Which may also serve for a full Answer to a late pamphlet entitled, Antinomianism Anatomized, under the name of John Sedgwick, being for the substance of it a mere extract out of the said Dr. Taylor.

*"Now we, brethren, as Isaac was, are the children of promise. But as then he that was born after the flesh persecuted him that was born after the Spirit, even so it is now."*
{Gal.4:28,29}

Printed for the Edification of the Faithful

ORIGINALLY PRINTED IN 1644

### COMPLETE & UNABRIDGED
### Supralapsarian Press
### 2014 EDITION

# THE ASSERTION OF GRACE;

or

The doctrine of Free Grace vindicated and defended against the calumnies and objections of Dr. Thomas Taylor in his Regula Vitae.

## Chapter I

≡≡≡≡≡≡≡≡≡≡≡≡≡≡≡≡≡≡≡≡≡≡

Dr. Taylor - Page 1 & 2: "It is to be inquired, what it is to be under the Law? Namely, not under the rule and obedience of the Law, for our Apostle looseth no believer from that; but believers are not under the reign of the Law; by the reign of which sin reigns unto death."

R. Towne: Surely it will not prove safe in the end to separate what God hath by his Divine and Absolute Authority conjoined; but to omit this your failing till a fitter time and place; for who knoweth not that ground less and vain distinctions have ever been coined to uphold a bad cause, to deceive and mislead the simple, and to serve for a cloak of a dis-honest mind, which to hide its nakedness is subtle in seeking subterfuges and evasions?
    I confess, that you walk but in the steps of many learned and judicious writers in this your expression; but yet when I considered, that they were but men who could not challenge the infallibility of an unerring spirit; that no Scripture could be produced to teach or warrant them thus to distinguish; but rather, in my slender skill the Scripture did oppose this practice. That it was a vain and causeless fear that occasioned this

needless shift. That the terms or parts {reign and rule} in propriety of speech, use of Scripture, or strictness of sense, do import and carry no true and real difference. Lastly, that it is utterly impossible, witness all true Christian experience, in practice to observe this distinction.

For; who is he that ever seriously seeketh God in the way of Humiliation and Repentance, {being the constant exercise of every believer,} and finds not first his inward mind and spirit, lying in great heaviness and affliction under the very reign of the Law; whereby sin reigns unto death; yea and that because he is conscious of his swerving from the straight and strict rule of the Law; and that his inward relief, ease, and reviving hath not been from the consideration of any conceived dispensation or abatement of power or rigor in the Law; but from the true and effectual apprehension of that plenteous redemption by Jesus Christ. {Rom.7:22,24,25} And how you vary from this distinction, ever and anon confounding the members, and overthrowing the whole of it, let the sequel of your treatise testify.

While I duly pondered, I say, these and the like reasons, I saw sufficient cause to dislike this interpretation, and to incline rather to their sense which understanding, by the word {Law} the moral Law or Decalogue, with all its authority, dominion, offices and effects, do also affirm that by Grace is meant alone the Gospel of Christ; and so will have the Apostle to ground this consolation, "that sin shall not have dominion" over them, in the adjunct state and condition of the Romans; thus reasoning in effect, if you were under the power and teaching of the Law, it's true, sin would then lord it over you, in that the Law is the strength of sin, "the sting of death is sin; and the strength of sin is the law;" {I Cor.15:56;} but you are translated into another Kingdom, where both sin, the enemy you so fear, is spoiled of all its armor and power whereon it dependeth; and also the King you now live under, doth freely communicate abundant and effectual grace of Justification and Sanctification, so to fence and fortify you on every side; that, in whatever siege or battle you be engaged, you may be more than Conquerors. Therefore fear not, nor be dismayed, only be strong in the faith thereof, so that your hearts may be encouraged in the Lord. The Law indeed called, and put you to fight against sin, for life and death; but it gave you no help at all, but rather insensibly and secretly it doth side with sin, that so it might work your overthrow and undoing. It strictly forbade all manner of sin under a heavy penalty; but the effect of this by reason of that native wickedness, and treachery of your corrupt hearts, was that sin more revived, increased, and enraged thereby, Rom.7:5, but now that your state is altered, the case is far otherwise.

And here I heartily with all diligence do mark some grounds or occasion of mistake, and misinterpreting this and many other parts, as namely; first, that Justification and Sanctification are separable, if not in the person, yet in regard of time; and the word of ministration, as if the Gospel revealed Justification, and the Law is now become an organ or an effectual instrument of Sanctification.

Secondly, that to ease men by faith of that intolerable yoke of the Law, is to leave and suffer them to range and run after the course of the world, and the fleshly lusts of their own hearts; not knowing or at last not duly considering, that the Righteousness of faith, unites them to Christ their Lord, Head and Governor, and so henceforth they may be led by his free Spirit, and swayed by the scepter of his Kingdom.

Thirdly and lastly, that all zealous and strict conformity to the Law of works, though but in the letter, is right Sanctification, whereas it is nothing so, as appears from Romans 9:31, 10:2, Phil.3:7, &c.

If any yet not perceiving these errors in these pharisaical legalists {for so more rightly may they be called than we Antinomians, &c.,} let him but note well the general and main bent of this treatise, and in it how falsely our tenents be propounded, how erroneously interpreted, how violently perverted, and what absurd consequences and carnal conclusions be hence inferred; by which his practice {I perceive and pity the Author's nakedness} he seeks to the uttermost to deface, discredit and extinguish both the sacred, saving, and most acceptable Truth of God, and the maintainers thereof, with intolerable and most unchristian terms, slanders and censors, that thus, if he want not of his will, both may be odious to all; which yet even in human policy, if I can judge, is not the way to obtain his desire, and he may soon be put out of doubt, that I suspect, or say not amiss.

Besides, his reason {to give you some instance and intimation what sufficiency is to be expected} which in the very entrance of his treatise, and of the opening of his text he gives, why the rule of the Law must not be meant, {which yet is without show of reason to a discerning mind,} doth argue what secret, blind, and sinister suspicions and causeless fears inclined him to this exposition; for, saith he, "our Apostle looseth no believer from that;" that is, from the obedience of the Law or Rule thereof. He dare not trust a believer to walk without his keeper; as if he judged no otherwise of him than that of a malefactor imprisoned at Newgate, who would run away, rob, kill and play his former pranks, if the jailer or his keeper be not with him when he is abroad. But who cannot see that whilst you thus overlook and refrain your disciples by your Moses, that they are only within compass by the Law, but are not true keepers of it.

But I muse that you omit to show what it is to be under Grace, which is the member and state opposed by the Apostle to this of being under the Law. Surely as there Paul is treating of Sanctification, and yet makes this antithesis before of being under the Law and Grace; so you could not have denied, that the Law must be taken comprehensively, with all his offices and authority; and that the reason is firm, that sin shall not have dominion over him who liveth under the Grace of the Gospel, because it hath a sanctifying virtue and power therein, to subdue sin, which the Law hath not. But you did wisely to pass it over, lest it should have raised your foundation and crossed your purpose; yet I wish that I be not mistaken, for I never deny the Law to be an eternal and inviolable Rule of Righteousness; but yet affirm that it is the Grace of the Gospel, which effectually and truly conformeth us thereunto.

≡≡≡≡≡≡≡≡≡≡≡≡≡≡≡≡≡≡≡≡

Dr. Taylor - Page 2: "Romans 7:6. We are delivered from the Law, being dead unto it, wherein we were holden; but who are those? It is those that serve in newness of Spirit, not in the oldness of the letter; that is, which now serve God in a new spiritual manner, excited and wrought by the Spirit."

R. Towne: "But now we are delivered from the law, that being dead wherein we were held; that we should serve in newness of spirit, and not in the oldness of the letter;" Rom.7:6; that is, which now serve God in a new spiritual manner, according to the operation of the Spirit of God, {for to serve in the oldness of the letter is, in that holiness which is only by the ministration of the Law, &c.,} which attending and accompanying the ministration of Righteousness, or the Gospel, {II Cor.3:8,9, Gal.3:2,} createth a new light, giveth the knowledge of the glory of God in the face of Jesus Christ, declareth his name and will, according to a New Covenant of mere Grace, without addition or mixture of works; and communicateth and distilleth the sweetness of the Lord's ravishing and overcoming love. {John 17:26} And thus swallowing up all former fears and discontentments, causeth in the believing soul, new thoughts, motions, and ways towards God different from whatever could be engendered by the ministration of the Law. {I Jn.4:18, Rom.2:15} Thus being dead to all opinions and concepts of God, and our own condition, according to our own worthiness or works, however wrought upon and made humble, devout, and conformable to the Law; conscience yielding and captivating herself to the same, the spirit is raised from death to life, delivered from bondage to liberty, and translated into another Kingdom of mere Grace and favor, only by the true and effectual apprehension of Christ and his Righteousness. {Rom.5:1,2,21}

Have you patience to see your halting and failing in the expounding of this Scripture, Rom.7:6, for the meaning is evident thus; that through faith in Christ is bred assured confidence, lively hope, pure love towards God, invocation of his Name without all wavering, fear, or doubting; not questioning his good will, audience, and acceptance; which could never be affected and attained by all the zeal and conscience towards God, according to the Law of works. And so the opposition is plain to be not so much between the gross hypocrite, {who is only brought to outward subjection and correspondency to the Law,} as it is between him that in good earnest and rightness of heart yields and gives over himself wholly to the Law of God, Rom.10:2, {as the wife to the husband and guide of her youth,} to be instructed and ordered in all things, inwardly and outwardly, after the mind of God therein, and so frames within himself concepts of God's will towards him, according to the testimony of his own legal conscience, {which never being satisfied with works can never be pacified and consistent,} and him who knows and worships God alone according to the Gospel of Grace.

≡≡≡≡≡≡≡≡≡≡≡≡≡≡≡≡≡≡≡≡

Dr. Taylor - Page 3: "It is the privilege of believers not to be under the Law, because Christ was made under the Law to redeem those that were under the Law that we might receive the adoption of sons, Gal.4:5, the reason is good; Christ was under the Law, therefore Christians believing are not under it; and Christians are redeemed from being under the Law, and therefore are no longer under it."

R. Towne: Read your four reasons again, and observe how ill they suit with and confirm your exposition of the text. How can this first assertion be good, unless you grant believers to be redeemed from the Law in that very same sense and extent that Christ was under it, as Mediator? But was not Christ under the rule and obedience also, {as you term it,} as well as under the reign to death, seeing that he came to do the will of his Father, and to fulfill all Righteousness. Matt.3:13.

≡≡≡≡≡≡≡≡≡≡≡≡≡≡≡≡≡≡≡≡

Dr. Taylor - Page 3: "As many as are under the Law, are under the curse, Gal.3:10, but believers are blessed with faithful Abraham, therefore not under the Law."

R. Towne: What frees the believer from the curse, is it not because by being a new creature {or creation} in Christ Jesus, he is first made personally, perfectly and everlastingly righteous, II Cor.5:21, Eph.2:10, Rom.5:19, Rom.8:4, Mt.5:20, the principal debt is obedience, the failing wherein bindeth over by virtue of Divine Justice to the curse and death. "For as many as are of the works of the law are under the curse; for it is written, Cursed is every one that continueth not in all things which are written in the book of the law to do them." {Gal.3:10}

=================================

Dr. Taylor - Page 4: "It is the privilege of believers to receive the Spirit of Christ, Rom.8:14, as many as are Christ's are led by the Spirit of Christ; and therefore they are not under the Law, Gal.5:18, if ye be led by the Spirit you are not under the Law."

R. Towne: Surely you were strangely taken and blinded when you thought upon these Scriptures? Rom.8:14, Gal.5:18. Do not both these places, as also your arguments from them tend to bring the believer from the ruling of the Law unto the government of the Spirit, even in sanctification or new obedience, although the Spirit that both cometh and worketh effectually in the dispensing of the word of faith, doth ever guide and bring forth fruits of Holiness and Righteousness according to the Law. Gal.5:22, Eph.5:9. I shall still be of that mind, that without Christ you can do nothing, nor be otherwise fruitful in one true good work, unless as a branch abiding in the Vine, you derive all your life, sap and goodness from Christ alone, Jn.15:4,5, which is by the

Spirit of faith. What if it be affirmed that even in true sanctification the Law of works is a mere passive thing, as the Kings Highway which a Christian freely walketh in? This you cannot deny or have any power to disprove. "I have stuck unto thy testimonies; O LORD, put me not to shame." {Ps.119:31}

===========================

Dr. Taylor - Page 5: "Consider the danger of being under the Law in four things. First, in that the Law wraps every sinner in the curse of God, both in this life and also in the life to come."

R. Towne: Whatever the Law saith, it saith to them that are under the Law. Rom.3:19. So that the head and chief danger of being under it, is, in that it reveals and requires such purity and perfection of obedience, and that without any jot of mitigation or favor, as it is to man utterly impossible. Mt.5:18, Gal.3:10. And thence is inferred your first danger in the second place, as a consequence of the former, to wit, that man failing to answer the first voice of the Law calling for such absolute holiness, he is then justly enwrapped as a transgressor in the curse of God, &c. But here it will be good and very useful hereafter to observe the right and proper ground and cause of this danger, which your words do in intimate and include, in that you say the Law wrapped every sinner, &c., so that whilst a man remains a sinner he is necessarily abiding under this fearful curse. The cause must first be removed before the effect can cease.

===========================

Dr. Taylor - Page 7,8: "Secondly, the Law in the reign of it shuts up heaven which receives no transgressor. Thirdly, it thrusts the sinner under the power of the devil as a condemned malefactor into the hands of the executioner to be ruled at his will. Fourthly, it addeth a sting and sharpens the point of all afflictions, which by it become the beginning of hell and its suitable curses."

R. Towne: To your second, third and fourth dangers, all that I say is, the Lord quicken and enlarge us all more effectually, and faithfully to use and apply the ministry of the Law for these ends and purposes.

≡≡≡≡≡≡≡≡≡≡≡≡≡≡≡≡≡≡≡≡

Dr. Taylor - Page 9,10,11: "Question. How may a man get from under this dangerous estate? Answer. By the attaining and exercise of three saving graces: faith, repentance and new inchoate obedience."

R. Towne: Give me leave to tell you, that this your prescription of the remedy against this danger is not Doctor-like. For it is neither sound, orderly, nor safe. For to let pass that which you improperly call these three graces, which are but gifts or effects of Grace, and that all the elect are saved in Christ, and ordinarily that have it exhibited and sealed in baptism, where they receive the kingdom of heaven as little children do their fathers inheritance passively. For that ordinance is a true, spiritual and real grafting of them into a standing in Christ. I Cor.12:13. So that Faith is but the revelation of what was secret, and hid before, or an evident testimony and lively and comfortable apprehension and application in the conscience of the person, of what was conferred and made his before. So that Faith works only a change as touching the conscience, whilst by an actual and sensible sprinkling of this blood on the doorposts thereof,

Christ purgeth, justifieth, saves; and causeth light there instead of darkness, life instead of death, liberty instead of bondage. Paul calls it the revealing the Son of God in him. Gal.1:16.

    I. It's not found, in that, whereas faith will admit of no other ingredient or partner in this business. Rom.3:28, Gal.2:16, Tit.3:5. You corruptly and treacherously do join and mingle repentance and new obedience with it in the very cause of Salvation and Deliverance from danger. Do you now walk with a right foot to the Gospel? Gal.2:14. Is this to teach healing and deliverance alone by Christ? Isa.53:5, Jn.3:14,15. Is this to preach a naked Christ, as Mr. Fox said? Must Christ be a lawgiver, an exactor of works in the very point of Justification and Repentance? Are you herein conformable and consonant to the established doctrine of our Church, which truly teaches free Grace, faith alone, only in Christ crucified, excluding and denying all works before and after, as physicians of no value, having no hand or stroke in this cure. See your face, Israel is stung with the fiery serpents, what remedy will you prescribe him? Will you bid him to look up to the brazen serpent, {weep and mourn, as he doth already in the sense of grief and danger,} that the LORD change his mind; and then promise the sinner stung by the Law healing upon these conditions? Or imagine, a man of an utterly decayed and impoverished estate lieth cast into a dungeon for a great debt, and you are sent unto him to tell him {as your only errand and message at this time} that all is satisfied, &c., and so bid him to be of good comfort, preach deliverance unto him, command him to come forth, acquaint him with the year of Jubilee, bid him go in peace and that all is forgiven him, and show unto him the undoubted testimony, and sure seal of these glad tidings; and thus, to receive, embrace, and to be not faithless, but believing; and will you be so unfaithful in your ministry, because of some needless suspicions and fears arising in your blind and natural heart {which can never be true to the doctrine of Free Grace} as if you saw danger, which God did not foresee, which will prevent you to presume in your own fancied wisdom to qualify, change and temper the message after your own humor, and tell him that although his Surety hath paid and discharged all indeed, but yet himself must weep and mourn, for his tears cannot but produce great effects, and will be sure so to affect and tender the heart of his Creditor that as soon as he knoweth how pitifully he taketh on, so instantly his bowels of compassion will so yearn, that he cannot contain or forbear any longer, but soon thereafter he will cross his debt book, cancel the bond and never charge him with anything hereafter. And also, this you must take as a necessary condition of release, that henceforth you have a care to cast to please your Creditor, and as your state increases again to be daily paying somewhat of your debt. When Peter and John healed the lame cripple, Acts 3:2, did they it by virtue of anything else than that of the only name of Jesus Christ of Nazareth, Acts 3:6, through faith in the same, set him sound upon his feet; or did they require also to further his soundness, that he must cry out, lament, leap and dance, and rejoice in the Lord? Are all these three {faith, repentance and obedience} necessarily required to the composition of your balm, or healing plaster; or have they all healing virtue in and of themselves? I am much ashamed in your behalf; but it can never sufficiently grieve and afflict my soul, that such untempered mortar, adulterated coinage, hotch potch divinity should pass pulpit and press without control, and be so generally received, approved and applauded. "The prophets prophesy falsely, and the priests bear rule by their means; and my people love to have it so; and what will ye do in the end thereof?" {Jer.5:31} Where may we find the incorruptibleness of faith, the simplicity that is in Christ? II Cor.11:3 The pure Doctrine of Justification freely by grace through the redemption that is in Christ Jesus? Rom.3:24. Oh, England beware of apostates! Let the fearful example of the unwise Galatians awake and admonish thee to take heed of false prophets, Mat.7:15, of evil workers, Phil.3:2, and deceitful men, II Cor.11:13, of corrupters of the word; II Cor.2:17; I mean such as to teach free grace, whilst fostering and maintaining that pestilent opinion that works also, and the keeping of the Law are necessary to salvation. Those are teachers of perverse things, Acts 20:30, that opposed the apostle Paul, and much pestered the church of Corinth, Galatia, Philippi, &c. Crafty they are in this, that directly, and in plain downright words speak not against justification in Christ; yet they do handle and carry the matter that their doctrine tendeth to the obscuring, defacing, and overthrowing of it. Oh the zeal of Paul in this case! What did he mean when he said, "Behold, I Paul say unto you, that if ye be circumcised, Christ shall profit you nothing; for I testify again to every man that is circumcised, that he is a debtor to do the whole law." {Gal.5:2,3} Is it not evident that the Galatians would not forsake Christ; yet they accredited that there must be an addition of something else to salvation, and what could be less hurtful to the Gospel than circumcision; yet see the effect of this conceit, as it separated them from Christ; they can have no benefit by him, and withal it draweth upon them the heavy yoke of the full and perfect observation of the whole Law. For the Law of works is so enwrapped and entwined together, that if a man lay hands on any, even the least link, he inevitably pulls the whole chain unto himself. And is not your conjoining of these three 'saving graces' {as you are pleased improperly and dangerously to call them, Acts 4:12,} that is, of faith, repentance and obedience to the Law, as much as circumcision, and can the consequences be less dangerous and damnable!

In a word, though enough can never be spoken against this pestilent, poisonous, and yet too common error; is not this that which brings in another gospel? Gal.1:6-8. You attribute something to Christ and faith, but something also to repentance and obedience; and this is impious and intolerable wickedness. "A little leaven leaveneth the whole lump." {Gal.5:9} This leaven, saith my author, is that false persuasion, that something is necessary to righteousness and salvation, besides faith in Christ; which soon will corrupt and spoil the whole mass of the doctrine of Free Grace; yea of the Gospel of Christ, as it maketh it the gospel of the devil.

True Faith may be compared to a mathematical point, which can admit of no addition or diminution; or to a gold ring, wherein the least cleft detracteth from the integrity of it. True faith bringeth nothing to God in the office or work of Justification and Redemption; but only sets the poor miserable lost sinner, taken captive and wounded to death by the Law, in the presence of God, naked, spoiled, and emptied of all goodness, strength, and hope, minding and apprehending alone the mere rich and free kindness and bountifulness of God in Christ Jesus, cleansing, clothing, healing, delivering and saving him from all danger whatsoever; and in a word, freely receiving him into His everlasting well pleased favor, and enriching him with all spiritual blessings in Christ Jesus. Thus are repentance, fear, hope, and love shut out of door, whilst this great work is in hand, though they always accompany faith in the justified. I hope it will not be denied by any rightly affected towards the truth, that faith is a judgment and persuasion according to the Gospel, the word of faith, whereof it is conceived and bred; so that, as the Law {being effectual} engenders fearful conceits and conclusions according to the true nature and office of it; so doth the Gospel on the other hand, set up a lively and joyful light of the knowledge of God in the face of Jesus Christ, {II Cor.4:6,} and only causes and raises such thoughts of God in the believer, as agree with that declaration of his loving and fatherly goodwill to us-ward in Christ Jesus, in whom God by his Gospel requireth nothing of man to salvation; but abundantly testifieth, and promises to do all himself, and so His promise is every way firm and free.

To this purpose observe diligently alone the words of Zanchi on Hosea 2:20, {"I will even betroth thee unto me in faithfulness; and thou shalt know the LORD;"} where he saith thus, "we are to note, that this is the simple and evangelical promise without any condition at all; for here God requireth nothing, but simply promises what he himself would do for his Church; insomuch as he promises faith also, without which the other promised, can have no place in us. Here is therefore a most perfect and absolute promise of all things which are necessary for his Church to Salvation. For he saith not, if thou wilt repent, I will receive thee into favor, and espouse thee; but absolutely, I will marry thee, &c."

Let all the world judge how unsound this doctrine of yours is, when as you shall never be able to show either from holy Scripture, the established doctrine of our Church, or any Orthodox writer, ancient or modern, that faith, repentance, and obedience, were ever made joint causes of man's freedom or deliverance from danger and misery; but contrariwise, that all and every of these do plainly and profusely deny any consideration and respect to be had unto anything as a cause, joint cause, effecting or procuring, or furthering our deliverance; save only unto faith in Christ, yea, and they do teach and maintain against all gainsayers that remission of sins, righteousness, peace, adoption, salvation, &c., are all the proper, immediate and sole effects or fruits of true faith in Christ our Lord. "Verily, verily, I say unto you, he that heareth my word, and believeth on him that sent me, hath everlasting life, and shall not come into condemnation; but is passed from death unto life." {Jn.5:24} "He that believeth on the Son hath everlasting life; and he that believeth not the Son shall not see life; but the wrath of God abideth on him." {Jn.3:36} It is never denied, but that true faith worketh by love, Gal.5:6, and is accompanied by good works, Eph.2:10; but what then, will you make love the form, ornament or in any way a help to Christ and Justification, or true blessedness. "But to him that worketh not, but believeth on him that justifieth the ungodly, his faith is counted for righteousness. Even as David also describeth the blessedness of the man, unto whom God imputeth righteousness without works; saying, blessed are they whose iniquities are forgiven, and whose sins are covered." {Rom.4:5-7} Or does faith know any object, beauty or ornament for the procuring of favor and acceptance with God than only Christ crucified, whom it apprehends and puts on, that it may be admitted into the Lord's presence, Rom.5:2; and so in every terror and conflict, it stills and pacifies the wounded conscience. Or dare you affirm that faith worketh any other work for the delivering of a man from the power of darkness than the bare and simple receiving of that abundance of Grace and the gift of Righteousness which resides in Christ alone? "And the grace of our Lord was exceeding abundant with faith and love which is in Christ Jesus." {I Tim.1:14} Why then do you thus inconsiderably, un-soundly and dangerously teach and write that something must be conjoined to Christ in the matter of our justification? Your eye is not without other members in the body, therefore will you conjoin your ears and hands with it in the office and act of seeing? But thus you deal, unless you hold that Justification is not sufficient to translate from sin and death to righteousness and life, unto which delusion, I hope you're not yet come? If you do not retract this for the sake of the Church, it will be aggravated by showing what abominable and intolerable evils will follow this doctrine. It defaces Christ, derogates from his sacrifice, obscures the Gospel, leaves the conscience always in fear and danger, spoils it of all peace, joy, and consolation, as it mingles Law and Gospel, and nourishes and maintains the special ground of Popery, engendering bondage, and is an enemy to all true godliness.

II. What order is this that you observe, that first faith apprehending Christ's Righteousness must go before legal Repentance? Also how indistinct are your lines, when you in effect make no difference between Repentance and Faith; for you call Repentance a turning to God which conversion is distinct from Repentance, Acts 3:19, and though the doctrine of our Church, as sometimes also the Scriptures do use the word 'repentance' comprehensively, as including faith also; how will this warrant and defend your course here, who do so professedly intend {or pretend} to separate by distinguishing words, what indeed, in nature, office and effects you conjoin or confound? How palpable also and dangerous to the simple is your oversight, in that you attribute to repentance, first to knock at the door of mercy, to seek and sue for pardon, not giving over till it have got a gracious answer, that sins are remitted. Secondly, to wipe off old scores, repeal all the actions of the Law, get all sins cast into the bottom of the sea. Have you forgot, being transported with blind passion or a zeal of the Law, that without blood-shed is no remission; Heb.9:22; or, that if you could weep a sea full of tears, yet they would be of no force or power to take away the least sin. For Christ by himself hath purged our sins. {Heb.1:3} And as touching conscience, only faith in this blood of Christ doth purify it. {Acts 15:9, Rom.3:25} You have, I think, outwardly subscribed to the established doctrine of our Church, which would have taught you truly, according to the word of God, that it is evident and plain, that although we be never so earnestly sorry for our sins, acknowledge and confess them; yet all these shall be but means to bring us to utter desperation, except we do steadfastly believe that God our heavenly Father, will for Christ's sake pardon and forgive us our trespasses, and utterly put them out of remembrance in His sight. Here you see that it is the alone office and effect of faith, apprehending the mercy of God in Christ Jesus. Mr. Calvin is of some authority and credit with you, and yet these be his words, "God holds us all at the staves end, to humble us, testifying that all by nature are utterly lost and damned, &c., secondly, that there is no soundness, nothing but corruption and abomination in us, and our ways. Thus it stands us upon, that God justifies us by his own mere and alone goodness, and look upon as singly in our faith, that we only rest in his promise. Let us leave therefore all things that men imagine to bring themselves into favor with God, by mingling this and that with faith; for they are all but falsehoods and illusions of Satan." {17th Sermon on Galatians, 1574} Calvin knew well {which experience cannot but tell you also} that blind and Popish conceits stick to men's hearts naturally closer than their skins to their flesh; to wit, if we could but get the heart to rent, tender and melt into tears, &c. If we could fast, and pour out our souls in great bitterness, and afflictions of mind, be enlarged in prayer, and holy duties, we should then hope, that God would hear and respect us; for this would much satisfy and ease the legal conscience.

If you wish to leave your colors, to forsake the Camp and cause of the genuine Protestant Doctrine, and to side with the adversaries, why do you yet complain that any should reprove you for it? Assure yourself, if there had not been too much ground and cause found in your ministry, and the ministrations of such who have mingled with you herein, you would not of had that allegation of monkishness and popery cast upon you; but by whomsoever you were so styled, {for I truly know not whom you mean,} I am sorry that you so justify and confirm their opinion.

Also, I now cease to marvel why you so oppose, calumniate and detest the simplicity of faith, and that good way of the Lord; though I still admire that so famous a city for the clear and distinct preaching and professing of the Gospel had none to admonish you of this your failing, before it was made so public. But names and commendations exceed the truth of our desserts. Also, I see that works still have many seeming friends, whilst few tender and regard what violence and wrong has be done to the doctrine of Free Grace. Yet it were somewhat more tolerable, if whilst you profess such friendship to the Law, you did not fall out of purpose to slander the Gospel.

III. Thirdly and lastly, how safe it is either for you to teach and publish this anti-Christian doctrine, making head and opposition thereby against the simplicity of Christ, or for your hearers, who have too servilely apprenticed their judgments to your teachings, as oracles from heaven; or yet for any other, {for its rare, and hard to keep and preserve the doctrine of grace pure without mixture,} I leave it to you, and the judicious reader to judge.

For if it be not by grace which is not in every sense grace; or if we be saved by grace without works of righteousness which we have done, Tit.3:5, {where note, that you be not deceived by such teachers, that by 'grace' is meant the alone Free Grace, and good will of God, by Jesus Christ, and not the gift of sanctification, which is always by Paul opposed to the free grace of God in the point and cause of justification and salvation, as Calvin saith,} whether then I pray you, doth this doctrine tend directly to obscure, destroy, and abrogate the grace of God or not.

≡≡≡≡≡≡≡≡≡≡≡≡≡≡≡≡≡≡≡≡≡

Dr. Taylor - Page 11: "Sincere obedience hath promise of acceptance with God, and is accounted as full and complete obedience to the Law."

R. Towne: Here you are too obscure and defective; for the righteous God loveth righteousness, Ps.11:7; the just and wise God who accepteth everything by due weight and measure, even as it is found to be, he doth not, nay he cannot simply account that which is but sincere and partial for full and complete obedience; neither can it stand with his absolute justice to accept anything which is not first perfect, seeing that perfection and absoluteness is the ground of acceptance both of our persons and performances. Either you are ignorant of the doctrine of Free Justification which maketh both the tree, and his fruit perfectly good before God, and is the salt of the Covenant wherewith every man, and every sacrifice that is presented to the Lord must be salted for acceptance; or else unfaithfully you put this candle, the only saving light of the Church under a bushel.

=============================

Dr. Taylor - Page 11: "And themselves now called perfect and undefiled."

R. Towne: By what, this creed of sincerity and obedience that you subscribe to?

=============================

Dr. Taylor - Page 11: "God looketh not now on their obedience as theirs; but as on his own work in them."

R. Towne: If as you imagine, first that there is some mitigation of God's justice by Christ towards his own people; secondly, that the ground of accepting their service is the working and worthiness of the Spirit within them, and not Christ's sacrifice and obedience without them; I pray that these places will let you see your error. "Ye also, as lively stones, are built up a spiritual house, an holy priesthood, to offer up spiritual sacrifices, acceptable to God by Jesus Christ." {I Pet.2:5} "Being filled with the fruits of righteousness, which are by Jesus Christ, unto the glory and praise of God." {Phil.1:11} Also, as their obedience, being the work of the Spirit in them; so it is passive to them, and is truly called the fruit of the Spirit. {Gal.5:22} And so it is an entire work and undefiled in every way correspondent only to the mind of the Efficient and Author, in agreement with the Law, as that rule by which he is engaged; but as it is still actively our obedience, so it is very imperfect and polluted; yea simply considered, it is as a menstruous cloth, Isa.64:6, and dung in the sight of the LORD, who is "of purer eyes than to behold evil," and cannot therefore not look on iniquity. {Hab.1:13} "Yea doubtless, and I count all things but loss for the excellency of the knowledge of Christ Jesus my Lord; for whom I have suffered the loss of all things, and do count them but dung, that I may win Christ, and be found in him, not having mine own righteousness, which is of the law, but that which is through the faith of Christ, the righteousness which is of God by faith." {Phil3:8-9} Also note here {good reader} how upon a false and erroneous ground that he hath himself now laid, he would build and bring in what afterwards, he would labor to deny and destroy; that is to say, God's not seeing sin in the justified. For God, saith he, "looketh not now on their obedience, as theirs." But, if God looketh not on their obedience now as theirs, how seeth he it defective unless you will hold God's work to be imperfect? Secondly, how then is God offended and angry with his children's failings; for both of those you afterwards affirm, but you seem little to mind or know what you write.

≡≡≡≡≡≡≡≡≡≡≡≡≡≡≡≡≡≡≡≡≡

Dr. Taylor - Page 11 & 12: "Question. How may we know a man is gotten from under this danger of the Law. Answer. By sundry notes and marks. First, by subjection to the Gospel in the power thereof."

R. Towne: I would here appeal to the conscience of any indifferent and judicious reader, as to just what he should mean by subjection to the Gospel in the power thereof? Surely, I mistake if he intend any other than the effects or fruits of the faith of the Gospel, and means not the faith of, in, or to the Gospel itself, which alone justifieth and saveth, unaccompanied with hope, love, or any other obedience in this office and act; and is that obedience alone that this doctrine calleth for at our hands, as sufficient to Salvation. "Verily, verily, I say unto you, he that heareth my word, and believeth on him that sent me, hath everlasting life, and shall not come into condemnation; but is passed from death unto life." {Jn.5:24} "But these are written, that ye might believe that Jesus is the Christ, the Son of God; and that believing ye might have life through his name." {Jn.20:31} "By which also ye are saved, if ye keep in memory what I preached unto you, unless ye have believed in vain." {I Cor.15:2} For only then are we out of danger when we are of faith, Gal.3:9, or are truly made obedient to the faith, Acts 6:7; that is, to that doctrine which proclaims faith in Christ unto Salvation. "Now to him that is of power to establish you according to my gospel, and the preaching of Jesus Christ, according to the revelation of the mystery, which was kept secret since the world began, but now is made manifest, and by the scriptures of the prophets, according to the commandment of the everlasting God, made known to all nations for the obedience of faith." {Rom.16:25,26} And as believing is called the obedience of the Gospel; so not to believe, or to refuse to hearken to the voice and call of the Gospel is termed the not obeying the Gospel, II Thes.1:8; and therefore you should have put and placed this for your first mark, whether a man be in the faith of Christ or not, II Cor.13:5; that is, whether he rightly understand, purely embrace, and solely rest confident in the doctrine of grace alone for justification and salvation without any addition or condition of works. Yea, whether when obedience of works faileth, and when he falls into sin, yet this grace of Christ be sufficient of itself to stay, succour and make confident the spirit and conscience. We can teach and learn that good works save not, and are confident whilst our own righteousness fails us not; but when will we teach and know that sins cannot "separate us from the love of God, which is in Christ Jesus our Lord." {Rom.8:39} This is that true Christian liberty, even the liberty of a purged and sprinkled conscience, Heb.10:22, which it is impossible that these yet should ever rightly learn, who conclude and infer thence a carnal licentiousness. Again, only to fear when we commit sin, and in our righteousness and holy walking to be secure is the fear of the hypocrites.

≡≡≡≡≡≡≡≡≡≡≡≡≡≡≡≡≡≡≡≡≡

Dr. Taylor - Page 13 & 14: "There is a peace of conscience from feeling sin pardoned, from perceiving sin subdued, and from discerning sin repented of, striven against and conquered."

R. Towne: Why rather place you not this before your thankful walking which is your second mark; but to testify how like yourself you will be, gathering security and peace rather from your repentance and reformation of life than by Justification by faith in Christ alone, which only is effectual to make and cause true peace and joy. "Therefore being justified, by faith we have peace with God through our Lord Jesus Christ." {Rom.5:1} "Now the God of hope fill you with all joy and peace in believing, that ye may abound in hope, through the power of the Holy Ghost." {Rom.15:13}

≡≡≡≡≡≡≡≡≡≡≡≡≡≡≡≡≡≡≡≡≡

Dr. Taylor - Page 14: "For the Spirit of Grace is ever a spirit of mourning and from this sowing in tears arises the harvest of joy."

R. Towne: To speak properly according to Scripture, it is the spirit of bondage that causes this mourning and sowing in tears which you speak of, after which in the elect flourishes the spirit of joy, but neither immediately, nor as an effect caused by heaviness or sorrow of mind; but only as it arises from the glad tidings of the Gospel being mingled with and received by faith.

≡≡≡≡≡≡≡≡≡≡≡≡≡≡≡≡≡≡≡≡≡≡≡

Dr. Taylor - Page 14: "The way to escape the yoke and compulsion of the Law is to become a free and cheerful observer of the Law, standing in three things. First, in a care to do the duties which the Law requireth, and in such a manner as the Law doth so near as we can."

R. Towne: Will you not cease to pervert the good and straight ways of the Lord? Doth our obedience or Christ imputed to us, free us from the yoke of the Law? Dost not the Son make us free? Is this to stand fast in the liberty wherewith Christ hath made us free, Gal.5:1, Jn.8:36, and to be not entangled again with the yoke of bondage? What blasphemy is this to derogate from Christ and to attribute what is peculiar to him through faith in his name to our own walking; yea, what wrong is this to the good Law of God to teach that a man may be free from its yoke, if he do the best that he can? What abusing of Scripture is this to uphold this pernicious doctrine? Doth the delight in the Law free the Apostle from the yoke or compulsion of it? Or had he his enlargement first from Christ by free Justification without works, the effect whereof was to run with great joy in the way of God's commandments. "I will run the way of thy commandments, when thou shalt enlarge my heart." {Ps.119:32} "Thou hast enlarged my steps under me, that my feet did not slip." {Ps.18:36}

≡≡≡≡≡≡≡≡≡≡≡≡≡≡≡≡≡≡≡≡≡≡≡

Dr. Taylor - Page 14 & 15: "Secondly, in humility and grief that we are so short of the Law in our best duties, &c."

R. Towne: Your humility and grief, because your obedience is so scanty and polluted is in itself a highway to sear your own conscience, and is under the very condemning power of the Law itself; for if they be menstruous works, are they not corrupt, abominable and damnable? What is this but to walk and live without faith in true Justification, which you profess to know and hold, but indeed deny, and to establish and bring in un-sanctified works or Popish contrition. For it is only Christ who is our Justification that sanctifieth both our persons and works. Your third, fourth, fifth and sixth marks are in effect all one, only some alternation there is in words and outward sound and form.

## Chapter II

*The sum of Dr. Taylor's Second Chapter.*

≡≡≡≡≡≡≡≡≡≡≡≡≡≡≡≡≡≡≡≡≡≡≡

Dr. Taylor: "To understand the Apostle's meaning, when he said, we are not under the Law; we are to know that this saying is not to be meant of the substance of the Law which standeth in these five things. That the Law is an eternal doctrine showing what is good and what is evil. Secondly, that it is a revealer of sin. Rom.3:19, 4:15. Thirdly, it is a rule of good life. II Tim.3:17. Fourthly, it is the express idea of the Law of nature written in men's hearts. Rom.2:15. Fifthly, it promises a righteousness and eternal life to all performers of it, which only, the believer expects, though in another way. But the Apostle only means that we are not under some circumstances and appendices of the Law; as, that it yolks every man to personal performance. Secondly, we are freed from the righteous exaction of personal and perfect obedience under pain of the eternal curse. Gal.3:13, Rom.8:1. Thirdly, we are freed from its urging itself upon the conscience with fear and terror. Fourthly, we are not under the Law for Justification. Rom.3:20. Fifthly, we are not under the Law as the minister of death. II Cor.3:7, Rom.8:1. Sixthly, the believer is not under the Law as exciting and provoking our corruption, rebelling against the Law, Rom.7:11, who by Grace is in great part freed from this resistance. Seventhly, as it is considered in the hand of Moses in regard of sundry circumstances, as time, place, persons, tables, testaments, manner, measure, terror, &c., in these regards believers are not under the Law."

R. Towne: Your labor is to be more subtle than solid, who so liketh the hunting of the Fox may follow you step-by-step. It shall content me to spy out and note your craftiness in seeking out witty, colorable and unwarrantable distinctions, which must serve hereafter for pillars or stays to uphold your tottering and weak tenents, and also for engines to fight against the Truth. Well may your abuse of Scripture, flourish of words and chiefly your cunning craftiness, make all you write and say to be acceptable with many; but the wise will try the spirits. "Beloved, believe not every spirit, but try the spirits whether they are of God; because many false prophets are gone out into the world." {I Jn.4:1} If a man may take liberty without true light and ground from God's word to distinguish and divide at his pleasure, he may pervert any truth, be it never so express and plain, as we see in the Romish Schoolmen;

unto whom therefore such unbridled license will not be granted by our Protestant antagonists; and the unhappy effect of such cutting and parting oft times is that the Truth in contention is maimed, if not quite overthrown and lost thereby.

Let me bring your own practice here for instance; as it pleases you to pick a quarrel against them that have done you no injury, to cast foul aspersions falsely upon them, to brand them with reproachful terms, to blaspheme them and their doctrine, Rom.3:8, to be too credulous in receiving unjust reports, and wickedly to pervert and misconstrue their sound and wholesome words; to let pass how uncharitable your dealing is in many ways, and how far swerving from that rule you perceive and labor to maintain; and how justly you have exposed yourself to that sharp reproof, "thou therefore which teachest another, teachest thou not thyself; thou that preachest a man should not steal, dost thou steal?" {Rom.2:21} I would have you in seriousness to let me see, now after your violent and injurious chopping and mangling of the inviolable and eternal Law of God, the true face, for me, and being of a Law. If it be true, that the Law cannot condemn, it is no more a Law saith Luther; and if there be no Law Divine {or human law, properly so-called} which is not furnished by the Author thereof with power, as to teach what is right, what is error, what is good, what is evil; to command the one and forbid the other; so to promise peace, security and good, that is, to justify the observers of it and to threaten, condemn and punish the transgressors of the same. "Cursed be he that confirmeth not all the words of this law to do them. And all the people shall say, Amen." {Deut.27:26} "For as many as are of the works of the law are under the curse; for it is written, Cursed is every one that continueth not in all things which are written in the book of the law to do them." {Gal.3:10}

Secondly, if the authority and power to command with promises and threatenings, as in a case a man keep and obey it, then to commend, justify and reward him; and if he offend, to accuse, condemn and punish him, whensoever he is tried in the Court of Justice, be the form constituting a Law, the absence or want whereof infers a nullity. What now is become of your Law, or where is it, produce it if you can? I say not that you have dealt as un-courteously with it, as did that king with David's servants, who cut off their garments by the midst, {"wherefore Hanun took David's servants, and shaved off the one half of their beards, and cut off their garments in the middle, even to their buttocks, and sent them away;" II Sam.10:4,} but you have done worse, for even Joab-like, {"and Joab said to Amasa, Art thou in health, my brother? And Joab took Amasa by the beard with the right hand to kiss him; but Amasa took no heed to the sword that was in Joab's hand; so he smote him therewith in the fifth rib, and shed out his bowels to the ground, and struck him not again; and he died;" II Sam.20:9-10,} under fair pretenses and friendly words, you have killed and destroyed the life and soul of the Law. Will you see this yet proved? Then mark well your appendices or consequences, as you term them, which you can as well separate from the Law, and yet let it remain a true Law, as you can take the brains and heart from a man and yet leave him a man still.

1. Can you suppose any to be under the mandatory and directive power of the Law, and yet the Law must not speak to him, not require personal performance at his hands, or bind him personally to obedience, for so you write. But the truth is, that until in your own person, you be a fulfiller of the Law, having the whole

righteousness of the Law in you, Rom.8:4, 3:22, you must remain in every kind under the utmost rigor, power and extent of the Law. "For I say unto you, that except your righteousness shall exceed the righteousness of the scribes and Pharisees, ye shall in no case enter into the kingdom of heaven." {Mt.5:20} You say that the Mediator hath fulfilled the Law on the behalf of his people; true, but unless you are joined to him and in union with him; {"he that is joined unto the Lord is one spirit," I Cor.6:17,} that is, a new creation in Christ, and thus completely and personally just and holy, you cannot be freed from the yoke of the Law. II Cor.5:17, Col.1:22; 2:10. You are wide still, for mercy through Christ delivers and saves none but in, and according to a due course of Divine Justice. Justice is not satisfied with me, until I be made and presented before it pure and blameless. Hence it is the necessity of the new birth, Jn.3:3, which is our being delivered from the power of darkness, and being translated into the kingdom of his dear Son, Col.1:13, {as Melanchthon expounds that place in John chapter three,} and so Master Fox {in his sermon of Salvation by Christ only} which regeneration gives us a standing in Christ. "To open their eyes, and to turn them from darkness to light, and from the power of Satan unto God, that they may receive forgiveness of sins." {Acts 26:18} "For ye were sometimes darkness, but now are ye light in the Lord." {Eph.5:8} "But ye are a chosen generation, a royal priesthood, an holy nation, a peculiar people; that ye should show forth the praises of him who hath called you out of darkness into his marvelous light." {I Pet.2:9} "For God, who commanded the light to shine out of darkness, hath shined in our hearts, to give the light of the knowledge of the glory of God in the face of Jesus Christ." {II Cor.4:6} Hence it is that every one that is saved will believe, be baptized and put on the Lord Jesus

Christ; and hence doth the established doctrine of our Church rightly teach that now in Christ, and by him, every true Christian may be called a fulfiller of the Law.

2. Your second appendix depends on this; for until everyone appear just in all points according to the first voice of the Law, it neither doth, nor can cease to curse and condemn him. Also when a believer is made the Righteousness of God in Christ, then the Law neither doth nor can curse. II Cor.5:21, I Tim.1:9.

3. If the Righteousness of faith be not in the conscience, you shall never be armed and fenced against the accusations and terrors of the Law. Rom.5:1, 8:33. Neither without this can you have the Spirit freely and cheerfully to incline you to the way of the Lord. Gal.5:6. "O that my ways were directed to keep thy statutes!" {Psa.119:5} "Make me to go in the path of thy commandments; for therein do I delight. Incline my heart unto thy testimonies." {Psa.119:35-36}

What is said may serve also for your other appendixes {that so I may avoid too much prolixity and tediousness} for they all stand and fall with the former. Fair words and glosses must not deceive us. The Apostle tells us, that "we know that what things soever the law saith, it saith to them who are under the law; that every mouth may be stopped, and all the world may become guilty before God." {Rom.3:19} He doth not mince and part the Law as your manner is. Moreover, do you not now see that these appendixes are essential parts of the Law, and are far more than the least jot or tittle, which yet is imperishable. "For verily I say unto you, till heaven and earth pass, one jot or one tittle shall in no wise pass from the law, till all be fulfilled." {Mt.5:18} Also I appeal to your own inward experience. Can you put your conscience under the mandatory, and yet keep it from the damnatory power of the Law? The Law saith, "love your enemies and bless them that curse you." When your spirits be dis-tempered upon any occasion and you be provoked to sinful anger, bitter and passionate speeches, shall you not feel this other consequence, namely, the effect and power of the Law condemning you for transgression? Why will you thus dally with the word? How dare you separate what God hath conjoined? How is it that you impose such impossibilities upon others? You might learn from that place, Rom.2:15, cited by you, that if the Law be not a bridle, it will prove a whip. If you hearken not to the direction of it in the conscience, it will then unavoidably charge heavily, accurse and condemn. So that Paul knoweth here no other, but that the damnatory power is inseparable from the Law; so every conscience teaches impartially, which is Lex Applicata {the Law applied.}

You speak of the substance of the Law in five sections; and I see and know nothing in all the Law, but what is substantial and essential, save that your last appendix, it may be, is something circumstantial. Also, in plain terms, I am of that mind, that the whole Law is in as full force and power as ever it was, and that nothing without damnable violation can be taken from it. Mt.5:19. But yet that believers should be under it, it is to me full of danger and contrary to all Scripture, and namely, to your text in hand. Let me deliver my mind, and then censure me. When I say, a believer, I mean one that is in Christ, and can never be separated or considered apart from Christ, {for then he ceases, at least to your thoughts, to be a Christian or believer,} one that is washed from all sin, made just and holy, the friend and son of God, the spouse of Christ, the heir of all things, the conqueror of all his enemies, advanced to sit and remain with Christ in the glory of heaven forever. He is neither male nor female, Jew or Gentile, &c. Gal.3:28. He is out of the power, kingdom, and limits of the Law; he is one spirit with Christ Jesus. I Cor.6:17. And to come to you, I demand, can he only know God now, and worship him, but by the ministration of the Law? The Scripture propounds God in Christ, and his righteousness to be known and worshiped by the believer. "For God, who commanded the light to shine out of darkness, hath shined in our hearts, to give the light of the knowledge of the glory of God in the face of Jesus Christ." {II Cor.4:6} "And all things are of God, who hath reconciled us to himself by Jesus Christ." {II Cor.5:18} "All things are delivered unto me of my Father; and no man knoweth the Son, but the Father; neither knoweth any man the Father, save the Son, and he to whomsoever the Son will reveal him." {Mt.11:27} "For in him dwelleth all the fulness of the Godhead bodily, and ye are complete in him." {Col.2:9} In Christ is the fullness of the Godhead, in him God is reconciling the elect unto himself, not imputing their sins; in him he is to be apprehended as their God and Father. Jn.20:17, II Cor.1:3. These treasures only faith discerns, attains and possesses in Christ. Hence is the peace, security, consolation, joy, contentment and happiness of the believer; but the ministry of the Law reveals not Christ, nor his Righteousness; Rom.3:21, it sets not forth God unto us, as a justifier of them that are of the faith of Jesus, Rom.3:26, as pacified and well pleased forever in him; Mt.3:17, it dispenses not the invaluable and unsearchable treasures of Christ, Eph.3:8; it declares not the name of God our Father in Christ Jesus according to the New Covenant of Grace, whereby the secret, sweet and incomprehensible love wherewith he loved his Son may be in us. Jn.17:26. But on the contrary the Law shows God to be a requirer of my righteousness, condemns me for my failing therein, having plagues, hell and destruction prepared for me because of my sins. Rom.1:18; 4:15. The fruit and consequence is that the conscience is robbed and deprived of all her joy, peace and consolation, and is filled with fears, terrors and confusion. Tell me now whilst you preach the Law of works, can you show me the condition, relation, name, happiness or face of a believer? In proper terms, doth the Law speak to a Christian or know any jot of Christianity?

But if you will put this man down, who even now walked by faith in the Son of God, had communion with God, I Jn.1:3, and his conversation in heaven, Phil.3:20, and will judge him as he converses on the earth, is seen of the world, &c., then as Luther saith of Moses when he came out of the Mount, you shall perceive him according to his power, carefully living and walking according to all the good laws of God and men, delighting in the righteousness of works, attending on his place and calling. Yea here, because his righteousness is defective and faileth, James 3:2, he is found to be a sinner, reproved, accursed and condemned. Thus is the old Adam and all his works shut up under the Law and Wrath of God. Here man stands and falls by his own works, is praised or dis-praised, justified or condemned, rewarded or punished.

Here if you will be a wise master builder, a faithful minister, a skillful workman that can divide the word aright, put a difference between things that differ, distinguish between Law and Gospel, the righteousness of works and faith, giving each their place, office and due; you need not be ashamed. I Tim.5:17. Let this suffice for the clearing of this chapter; in the closure whereof it pities me to see such opprobrious and unchristian-like epithets and titles; and your weakness of sight and want of power to manage and maintain what you have undertaken.

# Chapter III

*Dr. Taylor's Third Chapter.*

≡≡≡≡≡≡≡≡≡≡≡≡≡≡≡≡≡≡≡≡≡≡≡

Dr. Taylor - Page 32: "Now because the sons of Belial are come out, and tumultuously are risen."

R. Towne: St. Paul complaineth of your fellows in this business, that they would be doctors of the Law, and understood not what they spake, nor whereof they affirmed. I Tim.1:7. I know, that the ministry of the Gospel, and the doctrine of Free Grace, could never yet be so wisely and cautiously dispensed by Luther, Paul, Stephen, &c., nay, by Christ himself, the Wisdom of God, but still it was thus charged and calumniated, and that by the zealous workers of the Law. And therefore let none think it strange, that it is our lot in these days. For as Christ's humble, pure and meek spirit liveth in his saints forever, so that envious, carping and falsely accusing spirit of the Pharisees will breathe on the earth till the worlds end. Sport yourself and play your pranks, abuse and revile us at your pleasure; only take heed, that the stones that you cast or the arrows of bitter words you shoot do not fall upon your own head. You draw us unwillingly into this field of contention, where though you mistake and transform us into strange and base shapes and similitudes, {as best befits your humor,} to expose us the more unto the contempt and hatred of the world; yet lest our silent should argue guilt or diffidence in our cause, or prove any way prejudicial to that invaluable Truth of God; in the name of our God, we would do somewhat to the further clearing and the just defense thereof. For aptly said, the Truth of God is of such value that his meekest servants will contest, and the mildest fight before it be damaged by their forbearance.

=============================

Dr. Taylor - Page 33: "Therefore we are to prove against them, that true believers have a true use of the Moral Law."

R. Towne: Against whom? I am persuaded that neither yourself, nor any of your confederates dare say that ever they heard one of an indifferent judgment and understanding {and it ill beseems the gravity of a doctor in divinity to scrape and receive whatever falleth from the illiterate and simple, and to bend all his forces, by study, pulpit and press to quell and confute the same} simply to deny the use of the Moral Law to true believers. For it keeps them close in spirit and conscience through faith unto Christ's Righteousness, and makes them to live in a continual forsaking of themselves, and in a neglect, a base esteem, and an abhorring of their own virtues and works in God's presence; though they shine gloriously in the same to others, as Abraham's and Paul's example teach and show. "For if Abraham were justified by works, he hath whereof to glory; but not before God." {Rom.4:2} "But what things were gain to me, those I counted loss for Christ. Yea doubtless, and I count all things but loss for the excellency of the knowledge of Christ Jesus my Lord; for whom I have suffered the loss of all things, and do count them but dung, that I may win Christ." {Phil.3:7-8}

=============================

Dr. Taylor - Page 33: "Besides their lively faith, wherein they have received the Spirit, they have need of the direction and doctrines of the Moral Law, for the performance of the duties thereof, and that by these reasons."

R. Towne: It's not denied, but as in civil things, the Civil Law; so in moral things, the Moral Law doth instruct and direct, but what is this now in the matter of Christianity? I know not where to learn my duty to my superiors but in the matter of the fifth commandment; nor what murder and adultery is, but by the sixth and seventh. Yet let me tell you, that if you apply and urge these or any other ever so earnestly with all your motives and means fetched from the Law, you can never hereby make me to keep them inwardly and indeed. But whilst you through hope of good or fear of evil may work a restraint hereby, and make me love God and my neighbor wickedly, as Luther saith, my heart doth in no wise embrace them. For how can the Law free or cleanse the heart from evil motions and thoughts, seeing faith only purifieth the heart, Acts 15:9, and the Law is not of faith. Gal.3:12. Or what other fruit is there of your legal ministration, than that you delude poor and simple souls, making them think themselves something when they are nothing, to esteem themselves observers of what, through the strength of inward concupiscence they violate unceasingly; or thus to make hypocrites, that is, your disciples to appear what they are not, like whited tombs. The Law is spiritual, our hearts be carnal; the only authority that changeth us is the Gospel, embraced in faith. Therefore doth the Apostle make faith unfeigned the root and fountain of all spiritual access to God in Christ. Faith maketh the conscience good and the heart pure, whence proceeds love, which is the end, the fulfilling of the Law; for it wrongs no man. I Tim.1:5, Rom.13:8,9. Faith includes all things in it, saith Mr. Calvin. The high and ready way to repentance and good works is the preaching of

Christ and Faith. Gal.5:6. Whilst I bid a man to believe, I bid him do all things, I bid him love, &c. In a word, you may show me much that I ought to do; but what is this, if you cannot sweetly incline and freely enlarge my heart hereunto? If I have not faith and love, I keep not the Law, though the Law may well keep me as a jailer his prisoner within compass, &c. You that cannot endure passiveness in its place, yet stand too much for it, where only the Active cause is needful.

≡≡≡≡≡≡≡≡≡≡≡≡≡≡≡≡≡≡≡≡≡≡

Dr. Taylor - Page 34: "Reason 1. If the same sins be forbidden after faith as before, then is the Law in some force to believers; for the Law only discovers and reveals sin, Rom.7:7, and sin is the transgression of the Law. I Jn.3:4."

R. Towne: Keep the Law and works here below on the earth; and as Enoch converse in spirit and walk with God in the alone Righteousness of Christ apprehended by faith, and you shall easily discern that though Justification be an individual act, perfected in an instant, and not by succession and degrees, as is inherent holiness; yet the virtue and efficacy of it is to clear the conscience, to erase all sins out of the book of God's remembrance, to keep the believer in everlasting favor, peace, security and perpetual happiness; so that though the Jebusite must be in the land, and the prick in the flesh, and the law of sin in the members, which incessantly forceth us to sin, more or less, inwardly or outwardly; yet faith discerneth this glorious Sun of Righteousness by his effectual beams and influence, perfectly purifying and perfuming the air that we live and breathe in, Gal.2:20, and banishing all the mist and vapors arising from these earthly members out of God's sight and presence. The justified lives by faith, Hab.2:4; thus I am a sinner, and no sinner; daily I fall in myself, and yet stand firm in Christ forever. My works fail, his works never can, and they also are mine. Christ's righteousness is everlasting, and so are all the blessed fruits thereof, as peace, joy, life, acceptance, reconciliation and salvation.

≡≡≡≡≡≡≡≡≡≡≡≡≡≡≡≡≡≡≡≡

Dr. Taylor - Page 36: "This argument our Novatians and Familists can by no other shift avoid, but by flying to a perfect purity in themselves."

R. Towne: When you can prove us Novatians and Familists, or ever to have taught or held perfect purity in the flesh, or can produce such a principle out of any Catechism of ours, as you mention, then we shall see what warrant you have thus to write; but until you make good your words by better testimony and evidence, I shall count them no better than uncharitable slanders and mere falsehoods. But whereas you say, "if the Law were indeed abolished, why should they not worship false gods, steal, swear, &c.," you hereby show how little experience you have of the true light, power and grace of Justification, the reign of grace in Christ, {"that as sin hath reigned unto death, even so might grace reign through righteousness unto eternal life by Jesus Christ our Lord, Rom.5:21,} and how rarely you behold and worship God in Christ Jesus, in whom alone he hath put his name and memorial there to be found and sought, that there he may meet with us, commune with us and bless us; as also that we may thank the Law, not you, that you do not steal, rob, stab, kill, &., if this be the true teaching and learning of Christ, or the right receiving of the Gospel of Salvation, let him judge that understandeth. "But ye have not so learned Christ; if so be that ye have heard him, and have been taught by him, as the truth is in Jesus; that ye put off concerning the former conversation the old man, which is corrupt according to the deceitful lusts; and be renewed in the spirit of your mind; and that ye put on the new man, which after God is created in righteousness and true holiness." {Eph.4:20-24} "For the grace of God that bringeth salvation hath appeared to all men, teaching us that, denying ungodliness and worldly lusts, we should live soberly, righteously, and godly, in this present world; looking for that blessed hope, and the glorious appearing of the great God and our Saviour Jesus Christ; who gave himself for us, that he might redeem us from all iniquity, and purify unto himself a peculiar people, zealous of good works." {Tit.2:11-14} What psychic you greatly need to purge such a vile, lustful and distempered heart, I see with much grief of soul, and earnestly do beg it for you at the throne of Grace.

≡≡≡≡≡≡≡≡≡≡≡≡≡≡≡≡≡≡≡≡≡≡≡

Dr. Taylor - Page 40: "Reason 2. The same duties be required of all after faith, as before, and every conscience bound to the performance thereof, and the Law is the rule of these duties, as appears in Christ's Sermon upon the Mount."

R. Towne: You play but the Sophister, and whether I should yet impute it to your ignorance or malice, I know not? I would know first whether all the duties towards God and my neighbor, which the Law as a covenant or bond between God and my conscience throughout all my life requires of me, be performed by Christ my Surety; and so through our Saviour's Suretyship engagements every believer is become a perfect fulfiller of all the righteousness of the Law in one instant. "That the righteousness of the law might be fulfilled in us, who walk not after the flesh, but after the Spirit." {Rom.8:4} Secondly, whether that Christ so establishing and vindicating, and opening of the spiritual intent and meaning of the Law in that Sermon, {Matthew chapter 5-7,} was especially, if not solely, that by so doing he might destroy all vain boasting and confidence in man's own righteousness of works, which was dangerously bred in men's minds by that unskillful and unfaithful use of the Law in the hands of the Scribes and the Pharisees, whilst he let them see how spiritual, perfect, and absolute the will of God is in his Holy Law; inasmuch that if there be but the least ataxia in the thoughts, ever so secret motion or lust to evil in the heart, it casts and condemns them to hell, and everlasting destruction; that by this means every man might see and learn how worthless whatever he could do was before God, and that notwithstanding all his zeal towards God, Rom.10:2, witnessed in all his strictness, and travail about mortification and holiness; yet he still remained as deep in condemnation as ever he was, and there was no difference of state or condition between him, and the vilest, and loosest, and worst of men. {Rom.3:19-23} That thus he might prick the vein, and let out the proud blood of all work mongers whose spirits be lifted up above others, as if their own care, watchfulness and diligence had anything bettered them. Secondly, that thus he might make the way plain, that none might stick in the Law of works by this deceitful and pharisaical ministration of it, and so be kept from Christ to their own perdition {from which no works can deliver and save,} but might be driven and compelled to run and hasten to him, and his righteousness to the everlasting security and salvation of their souls. Thus God in his Law would have all men kept at the staves end, because he receiveth none into his favor and kingdom by any other way or means than by faith in the obedience of his own Son; and though the Law be established also in our sanctification, yet it is in the inward spirit, not the outward letter, it is from the Law written in the heart, and not engraven in tables of stone, it alone issues from the lively spring of free Justification joyfully apprehended in Christ, and not from the outward dispensation and precepts of the Law. "For the kingdom of God is not meat and drink; but righteousness, and peace, and joy in the Holy Ghost." {Rom.14:17} "For the kingdom of God is not in word, but in power." {I Cor.4:20}

    Lastly, notwithstanding all this inherent holiness and newness of life; yet the believing soul and the affections of the believer be dead to it in God's presence, and only have confidence in dealing with him through the Righteousness of Christ.

    This I trust, will sufficiently speak to the world for our just defense against all malevolent cavils and calumniations, and let all clearly see, that the doctrine of Free Grace only reconcileth God and man, the law and the conscience, and man and man; gathering and uniting all in the bond of love, flowing from the love of God shed abroad in the heart by the Spirit, Rom.5:5, in the ministration of the Gospel, Gal.3:2; and that whosoever labors to bring in works any other way does err; and though by their daily legal pressing, they put men to much and sore travail, yet the Law in their affections is loved and liked just as much as the taskmasters in Egypt were by the Israelites. For if those who are now hot and forward were left to themselves to live as they list, with promise and warrant of security from danger, their courage I fear would soon cool and abate.

The rest of his reasons might well have been spared, save that he loveth to please himself and to push recklessly at others, for I find nothing but fruitless repetitions of what is already said and answered; yet as we pass to the fourth chapter, note by the way, how he alleges a sentence out of Augustine, and another out of Ambrose, both which tend only to establish the doctrine of the Law in Free Justification, and not in sanctification as he pretends, and falsely rendering the former clause of Ambrose of purpose to make them speak to his liking, for he saith that faith shows those duties to be done which the Law commands to be done; whereas he should, if he had dealt faithfully, thus said, because what things are appointed in the Law to be done, by faith those are showed or declared to be already done; which is, that the doctrine of the Gospel testifies, that the Law is fulfilled to our hands; but in this eager pursuit of this pleasant argument he forgets himself and perverts all, as may most conduce to his own end.

# Chapter IV

*Dr. Taylor's Fourth Chapter.*

≡≡≡≡≡≡ ≡≡≡≡≡≡≡≡≡≡≡≡≡≡

Dr. Taylor - Page 60: "We will lay open the true grounds of this unhappy schism and the right use of these palpable errors; and these I observe to be three. 1. Gross ignorance. 2. Swelling pride. 3. Love of licentiousness, with the hatred of holiness, &c."

R. Towne: Here omitting the vain and vile spawn of a passionate and dis-tempered spirit, I note first that his three grounds of this supposed and miscalled schism; where if by "hatred of holiness" he meant that holiness, that righteousness and holiness of faith by which alone Christ makes and presents his Church holy, unblameable and without fault in the sight of God? "And you, that were sometime alienated and enemies in your mind by wicked works, yet now hath he reconciled, in the body of his flesh through death, to present you holy and unblameable and unreproveable in his sight." {Col.1:21-22} According to our creed, I believe a holy catholic Church; I would then stand to the censure of any judicious and impartial judge, upon whom in this point of controversy, these and every one of them might most deservedly be charged; and here again he takes a vagary, as unbridled lust leads him, and thus exposes his leanness, since his words I hope are but paper shot, and in the end will prove a slander. He can endure but little, who cannot patiently digest a few rash and disdainful words from one who professes and proclaims such love to their persons in the end of his preface to the reader; but yet having gotten hereby some new strength and courage, I mark with what insinuation he returns, promising such fair play, as that he will charge us with nothing but our own writings. {pg.63} Well, we shall surely know and own every one of his own hand when he sees it.

    Secondly, he seeks to breed and engender a harsh and hard conceit of his adversaries in the hearts of his hearers, thereby to prevent all reply of theirs, or at least all manner of credit to the same; for who dare believe them, who, upon a Doctor's word, are no better than gypsies, jugglers, cheaters, &c. And observe his enclosed reason, "for what can hold them, whom God's Law cannot," as if he knew no better preservative against sin than the Law; or as if it could keep any from the spiritual and inward breach of it; or to give all, to take notice how his sanctification is bread, and what a forced and undesired brat it is.

Lastly, to seal his testimony for an undoubted truth, he brings in a story and pretty passage, as current coin as the rest. I had made some inquiry, and am credibly informed, that it is a fable and untruth; and if that man be the author who was named to be, I say, that he is a right dissembler, for somewhat which I know. But thus it fared with the world. Let who will tell anything against such as they approve not of, his authorities shall be sufficient warrant to receive and preach it as a sacred oracle in the presence and place of God himself.

========================

Dr. Taylor - Page 65: "It shall not much trouble me, whether they own them or renounce them; as I avow them to be errors."

R. Towne: I fear of your own making them; for the authors, or some of them, {if you deal candidly, faithfully and punctually in propounding them,} are ready to justify and defend them against whatever you can bring to oppose and repel them.

========================

Dr. Taylor - Page 65: "Error first and second, that Christ came to abolish the moral Law; and that the Gospel takes away all obedience to the commandments and that true faith stands at defiance with working and doing. Error 2. That a godly life has nothing to do with keeping the commandments."

R. Towne: To the first and second error, I say, that they are so absurd and grossly false, that you shall give me leave, not to believe that ever you can show them under any man's hand, of any mean understanding in religion. But if you do, I shall willingly give you my best helping hand to confute and suppress them; though methinks their own nature and palatable ugliness and gross vileness, do sufficiently reprove and condemn them without our effort.

≡≡≡≡≡≡≡≡≡≡≡≡≡≡≡≡≡≡≡≡

Dr. Taylor - Page 72: "Error 3. That blessedness is merely passive, and therefore it is in vain to put men upon actions for that end."

R. Towne: The two former assertions and this one are ill matched and linked together; for those are not more vile and hateful, than this is fair and Orthodox, till it be blasted and corrupted with your own unsavory breath. I should scarce have been drawn to believe, that any professed Protestant divine {much less a Doctor} would ever have objected against this so sacred, sound, weighty and so clear a truth, so generally received and confirmed by almost all Orthodox writers. I will not say the cause is, that he is transported through pride or passion into raptures and fits next to lunacy and madness, or that this wisdom is not from above. James 3:14-18. I say, that by some occasion he hath much forgot and overshot himself, or else is minded to dis-taste and condemn anything, be it never so true, because of the hatefulness of their persons in his eyes. But what ground does he lay or pretend? His reasons alleged to be as weak as water; in effect, as if he had said nothing, save what blindness and ill-will he hath thereby bewrayed. Yet because this is of great and necessary consequence, and a point that calls for a challenge justly, a distinct, diligent and judicious search, knowledge and consideration, especially in these times wherein it is so much spoken against, almost in every pulpit, and all men earnestly are excited and pressed to an active righteousness of works, as if happiness did consist therein. I think it my duty to take a little pains, first in explaining the terms; secondly, in the confirmation of it by Scripture and human testimony; thirdly, and then I shall return and see what strength is in his arguments.

First, blessedness is a passive; that is, in the sense of Scripture and all true divinity, it consists alone in what God in Christ Jesus freely worketh and conferreth, without either works or worthiness in man. Justification and blessedness go for one and the same in Holy Writ. "Even as David also describeth the blessedness of the man, unto whom God imputeth righteousness without works, saying, Blessed are they whose iniquities are forgiven, and whose sins are covered. {Rom.4:6-7} And as divines rightly say, at the most they can but differ as to the antecedent and consequent, or the cause and effect; the one, that is, Justification, including the other, that is, blessedness, as the fire or sun doth heat and light. So that if Justification be passive, it necessarily follows that true blessedness must needs be so too; but Justification is passive, for it is God's act alone. "To declare, I say, at this time his righteousness; that he might be just, and the justifier of him which believeth in Jesus." {Rom.3:26} Justification is not the office of man but of God; or man cannot make himself righteous by his own works, either in whole or in part; for that is the greatest arrogance or presumption of man that antichrist could set up against God.

Secondly, God is not induced or moved by the consideration of anything in man, to give or impute this righteousness of his Son unto him, but justifieth him freely by his sheer Grace. "Being justified freely by his grace through the redemption that is in Christ Jesus." {Rom.3:24}

Now can anything fall to man more passively, than that God alone should confer and work righteousness and salvation himself, and that freely and fully without any respect or addition on man's part? If a poor wretch {that never could get a farthing by any labor,} should by the undeserved bounty of his Prince, have great treasurers and possessions bestowed upon him, and so presently become rich; is it not that this happy condition is passively attained. Or was man's blessedness passive in the first creation anymore than in his re-creation, regeneration, or justification. "For we are his workmanship, created in Christ Jesus unto good works, which God hath before ordained that we should walk in them." {Eph.2:10} "For it is God which worketh in you both to will and to do of his good pleasure." {Phil.2:13} "But we are bound to give thanks alway to God for you, brethren beloved of the Lord, because God hath from the beginning chosen you to salvation through sanctification of the Spirit and belief of the truth; whereunto he called you by our gospel, to the obtaining of the glory of our Lord Jesus Christ." {II Thes.2:13-14}

All that can be objected against this with any force or color of argument that I see, is either first, that Justification is blessedness only in part and not in the whole. For to a full and absolute blessedness is required also reconciliation, adoption, sanctification and glorification, unto which I answer; first, that if God only do work and perfect all these himself for man of the like Free Grace, then surely man's happiness is still passive; but it is plain that God alone is the author of all these, and of every of them. "And all things are of God, who hath reconciled us to himself by Jesus Christ." {II Cor.5:18} "A man can receive nothing, except it be given him from heaven." {Jn.3:27} "For of him, and through him, and to him, are all things;

to whom be glory forever. Amen." {Rom.11:36} "But of him are ye in Christ Jesus, who of God is made unto us wisdom, and righteousness, and sanctification, and redemption; that, according as it is written, he that glorieth, let him glory in the Lord." {I Cor.1:30-31} "But to us there is but one God, the Father, of whom are all things, and we in him; and one Lord Jesus Christ, by whom are all things, and we by him." {I Cor.8:6} "It is the same God which worketh all in all." {I Cor.12:6} "For by him were all things created, that are in heaven, and that are in earth, visible and invisible, whether they be thrones, or dominions, or principalities, or powers; all things were created by him, and for him; and he is before all things, and by him all things consist." {Col.1:16-17} See likewise; Rom.5:10-11; Phil.1:6; Phil.2:13; Ezek.36:25-27; Jer.32:39,40; Rom.8:30; Eph.1:3; Tit.3:5-6, &. If you add union into Christ, then it is God that baptizes by his Spirit into Christ. "For by one Spirit are we all baptized into one body, whether we be Jews or Gentiles, whether we be bond or free; and have been all made to drink into one Spirit." {I Cor.12:13} "For as many of you as have been baptized into Christ have put on Christ." {Gal.3:27} "I am the true vine, and my Father is the husbandman." {Jn.15:1} Further, God giveth his Son and opens the heart and bestows power unto all that receive them. "But as many as received him, to them gave he power to become the sons of God, even to them that believe on his name; which were born, not of blood, nor of the will of the flesh, nor of the will of man, but of God." {Jn.1:12,13} And if we have Christ then have we with him and by him all good things whatsoever we can in our hearts wish or desire, as victory over death, sin and hell; we have God's favor in Christ, and with him true holiness, wisdom, justice, life and redemption; and we have by him perpetual health, wealth, joy and bliss everlasting. Also Luther truly exhorts, "hold this firmly, that thou art not to do good to God, but only to ask, seek and receive by faith all good of him the fountain of goodness; Christ hath done all things for thee, only be contented with him, and thinkest by what means thou mayest get him to dwell more and more in thee, and strengthen faith; and then shall thy works be good indeed, when they profit others and not thyself, in that thou needest them not, seeing Christ hath done all for thee, and hath already given thee whatever thou canst either wish or seek, whether for this life or for the life that is to come." Also as is the cause, so is the effect; but Justification which is the sole, proper and immediate cause of all and every one of these benefits is altogether passive, as is already cleared.

Secondly, or else these weak grounds the doctor stands upon may be urged, as, that to believe is requisite to happiness; but to believe is an act, therefore, some action is requisite, and consequently blessedness is not passive only, neither is it in vain to put man upon some action for that end. Unto which I may shape this answer, that all that was either said or intended in that sermon, in which this so gross and damnable an error {if we may take your bare word for it} was uttered, and taken up by him that shrouded himself in darkness, as being afraid or ashamed to come into the light, much more being so devoid of all charity and humanity, that he never admonished, nor reproved the author for it, was to set receiving and doing, believing and working in opposition in the cause of true blessedness, after the example of the Apostle Paul. "So then they which be of faith are blessed with faithful Abraham. For as many as are of the works of the law are under the curse; for it is written, Cursed is every one that continueth not in all things which are written in the book of the law to do them." {Gal.3:9,10} "But to him that worketh not, but believeth on him that justifieth the ungodly, his faith is counted for righteousness. Even as David also describeth the blessedness of the man, unto whom God imputeth righteousness without works, Saying, Blessed are they whose iniquities are forgiven, and whose sins are covered." {Rom.4:5-7}

But, since this is held in your and his judgment so erroneous that your charity puts you upon this extreme, I add {in defense of that tenent against all that condemn or oppose it and especially against your first reason,} that faith as an act justifieth not, nor as it is a quality, virtue or work, doth it come within the compass of Justification. For to omit that passive receiving {like as infants receiving their fathers inheritance in a mere passive manner} mentioned in Matthew 18:3, &c., and even intimated in baptism, where the child's face is washed or sprinkled by the minister, and the Spirit inwardly and invisibly pours clean water, as a symbol of the cleansing efficacy of the precious blood of Christ, and the only way of access to the Father. To let this pass, I say {which yet would suffice to justify this tenent against you} although in the court of conscience, faith doth work in apprehending or receiving; yet this very acting or working of faith about this Object is excluded out of Justification, and as faith is said to justify, it is a passive work. Also Zanchi in Ephesians 2, alleges Bucer thus, that faith justifies not actively, but passively, because in Justification it gives nothing, but only receives, and we are justified with that very thing which it receives. It is the virtue of the plaster that heals, not simply the act of applying it.

Thirdly, if faith were admitted as it acteth in to the point, yet it also is the gift and work of God, as you will yourself confess. "For by grace are ye saved through faith; and that not of yourselves, it is the gift of God." {Eph.2:8} "Therefore said I unto you, that no man can come unto me, except it were given unto him of my Father." {Jn.6:65} Yea, and not only the habit or first beginning of it, but also the very action of that habit or quality; the preservation, continuance and consummation of it is of God, who worketh all our works in us. "LORD, thou wilt ordain peace for us; for thou also hast wrought all our works in us." {Is.26:12} "I will cry unto God most high; unto God that performeth all things for me." {Ps.57:2} "Being confident of this very thing, that he which hath begun a good work in you will perform it until the day of Jesus Christ." {Phil.1:6} "Now the God of peace, that brought again from the dead our Lord Jesus, that great shepherd of the sheep, through the blood of the everlasting covenant, make you perfect in every good work to do his will, working in you that which is well-pleasing in his sight, through Jesus Christ; to whom be glory for ever and ever. Amen." {Heb.13:20-21}

≡≡≡≡≡≡≡≡≡≡≡≡≡≡≡≡≡≡≡≡≡≡≡≡

Dr. Taylor - Page 72: "We are mere patients in the causes of blessedness, but in respect of conditions we are not so; for as we said of faith, we may also say of good works, God enables to do them, but man works them, and walks in the way of them to blessedness; not that our works are causes, but conditions, without which blessedness is not attained. Mt.25:35."

R. Towne: How unsound and un-Protestant like is this second ground upon which you seek to condemn this sacred and inviolable truth! What Scripture or approved writer have you for what you here affirm? It had been equal dealing, that first you had put the author of this foul error to an explanation of himself, and then if he had jumped with your sence here expressed, I grant he had deserved a sharp reproof and censor. I hope this is but one doctors opinion, for it is a pity that our Church should have many of your mind. The wise will first read and ponder, then judge.

If we be justified when we were ungodly, Rom.4:5, and that freely by Grace, Rom.3:24, without works, Rom.3:28; also if we be saved without works, Tit.3:5; yea, and first be saved and partakers of blessedness before we can do any good works, Gal.3:9, which plainly show that in order of nature; first, Justification, Salvation and Blessedness are attained by Christ and unveiled through the Gospel, and that then faith follows and floweth thence as an effect or consequence in the justified, saved and blessed. Then good works cannot consist or stand in competition with faith, either as causes or conditions in the compassing of true happiness. For how can they possibly be required as necessary conditions towards the attaining of that which is effected and possessed before they can come into presence, or yet have any being at all. That this is Paul's method, first Grace bringeth salvation, and then teaches us to deny ungodliness. Tit.2:11-12.

To prevent all evasions and to clear this point a little better; faith worketh two ways. First, as it is conversant about the glad and happy news of the Gospel, and here it rightly knoweth Christ, truly receiveth him, as the richest gift of the Father, and in and with him is made a possessor of all his unsearchable treasures, Eph.3:8, as remission of sins, Col.2:14, righteousness, II Cor.5:21, adoption, Gal.3:26, favor, peace and fellowship with God, Mt.3:17; Rom.3:25; I Jn.1:3, and eternal life, I Jn.5:11,12. Thus Christ first saves a man from all his sins, from wrath, death and the devil; and consequently banishes all former fears, torments and apprehensions of evil; and then putteth him into a present possession of all blessings in Christ. For so saith the Apostle; "for all things are yours; whether Paul, or Apollos, or Cephas, or the world, or life, or death, or things present, or things to come; all are yours; and ye are Christ's; and Christ is God's." {I Cor.3:21-23} Hence faith breeds peace passing all understanding, Phil.4:7, joy unspeakable and full of glory, I Pet.1:8; because our lines are fallen in so good a ground, or in that a believer is advanced unto such a present, Eph.2:13, full, Col.2:10, and everlasting condition. Jn.5:24. Now this first principle and most acceptable work of faith is accomplished, whereby the soul hath gotten victory over all her enemies, and is made heir of all things with Christ, Rom.8:17; for although faith continueth its act and fruition, causing the soul ever to dwell in joy and to live happily upon this heavenly inheritance; yet the former act of coming unto Christ, of acquisition or attaining hereunto is passed and done; and although faith be most diligent in the means of faith to receive a daily increase, whereby the heart and spirits be enlightened and enlarged to a more clear discovery and view, and to a more effectual and full apprehension; yet this enlightening or perfection of faith is exclusively God's gift and act. "For it is God which worketh in you both to will and to do of his good pleasure." {Phil.2:13} "Wherefore also we pray always for you, that our God would count you worthy of this calling, and fulfil all the good pleasure of his goodness, and the work of faith with power; that the name of our Lord Jesus Christ may be glorified in you, and ye in him, according to the grace of our God and the Lord Jesus Christ." {II Thes.1:11,12} So that in the use of means we are agents, but in respect of success only patients. Even hypocrites and reprobates may be diligent in the means, and yet not attain one jot of true felicity. "Strive to enter in at the strait gate; for many, I say unto you, will seek to enter in, and shall not be able." {Lk.13:24} "So then it is not of him that willeth, nor of him that runneth, but of God that sheweth mercy." {Rom.9:16} All this adds not to the good things, or the Covenant itself; as Israel travailed forty years with much pain and hazard to come to Canaan, and being there they acquainted themselves more perfectly from day to day with the nature, profit and pleasantness of their possessions; and a child grows up both in understanding and true estimation of his lands and revenues, but neither of their estates be enlarged or bettered thereby.

Secondly, then faith begins also to work by love, Gal.5:6, both towards God in loving him, {who first loved us undeservedly,} and ever rejoicing before him according to his great goodness, and magnifying his great name for such exceeding bountifulness and advancement, Lk.1:46, as also towards our neighbors, Gal.5:14; and the more that faith is rooted and grounded in the former, {as a tree planted by the waterside,} the more will it be fruitful and flourish in all newness of life; so that no doctrine, no not of the Law itself is so powerful and effectual to make a true Christian fruitful and abundant in all good works, as is the doctrine of pure and free Grace. To this Mr. Fox saith, that it is the office of Christ to justify in heaven, and so the nature of faith is here on earth to work by love, as a root doth by the sap. For as a man sees and feels by faith the love and grace of God towards him in Christ his Son, so begins he to love both God and man, and to do to his neighbor as God hath done to him. And, Mr. Tyndale, that Apostle of England agrees hereunto, affirming that the spiritual take heaven as the gift of God through Christ's accomplishments; they look on the exceeding mercy, love and kindness which God showed them in Christ, and therefore love and work freely. It would not be difficult to bring a full jury of Orthodox learned and approved authors, all affirming that Life and Salvation be promised and attained through the merits of Christ, by faith of the Gospel freely without condition of works. It is very strange to me, that either you should be ignorant of it, or whilst you oppose not us alone, but them also herein, that yet you should presume to have your word taken for the contrary, without better warrant than here you show.

Observe what may be said against you moreover, for if good works be such necessary conditions, that without them salvation is not attainable; then, though the Grace of God in Christ Jesus does save, as the alone cause of a believer's salvation, yet it doth it not freely. For what God doth freely, it is without all conditions or consideration of mans worthiness or works; for this know that whilst you teach the contrary, you do no other than make works to be the cause of salvation. If Salvation depended on condition of our good works or dignity, it would be uncertain and doubtful. "Therefore it is of faith, that it might be by grace; to the end the promise might be sure to all the seed." {Rom.4:16} You confound Law and Gospel, and run into that common error of men who hold that the Gospel is a conditional promise. But our minds ought to be withdrawn from such thoughts; and we are to know that the promise which is proper to the Gospel; namely, of remission of sins, reconciliation and of giving eternal life, doth not depend upon condition of works. Know also that hereby you accord with, and strengthen that natural knowledge and opinion that men have of God, namely, that he will freely justify and save none that are unworthy and unclean; and hence every natural conscience doth require a condition of some worthiness in man, that he may be saved, as doth the Law of works; but the Gospel fights against both of them and persuades the heart, that God for Christ's sake doth forgive and bless the unworthy freely. Hence it will follow {in accordance to your persuasion} that Justification or Imputed Righteousness is not sufficient to make men capable of Salvation unless they be also qualified and prepared by good works; so that a good and godly life fits us for heaven, and the more holy our life is, the fitter it makes us for that place, credit you who will; but I have learned of Paul to bless God, who hath already by free Justification and Adoption made us meet to be partakers of the inheritance of the saints in light. Col.1:12. For if our good works were the fitting of us, he would have rather said that we were a making fit, than that God himself hath made us meet; and lastly, then none are blessed before death; for whilst he liveth, man is but in the way journeying to salvation; yet Paul saith they that are of faith are {not that they shall be, by walking in good works,} already blessed in Christ. "Not by works of righteousness which we have done, but according to his mercy he saved us, by the washing of regeneration, and renewing of the Holy Ghost; which he shed on us abundantly through Jesus Christ our Saviour; that being justified by his grace, we should be made heirs according to the hope of eternal life." {Tit.3:5-7} Note that it is according to his mercy that he hath saved us.

You seem to befriend Luther, then consult with him in his sermon upon Titus 3:5, and see how you two accord. "It is a wonder, saith he, how the truth of these words can stand, in which the Apostle preaches that we are already saved, although living as yet on the earth, and therefore in continual misery; but thus he hath spoken, that he might more fully express the power of

Divine Grace, and the nature of true faith against hypocrites, who as though Salvation were yet afar off, in vain go about to bring it to themselves, and to get it by their own works. Verily, Christ hath saved us already two manner of ways. First, he hath perfectly done all things that are requisite to make us safe, &c. Secondly, he hath bestowed upon us all blessings in Christ, that whosoever shall believe that Christ hath perfected these things, in the same moment he might also have and enjoy them. So that no other thing is henceforth needful to Salvation but faith alone to believe firmly that all these things are thus made perfect." A little after, he says, "for it is meet that we have heaven, and be saved before we can do any good work at all; therefore the whole life of a believer after baptism is nothing but an expectation of salvation and felicity to be revealed, which they that do believe in Christ now do possess though covered and hid in faith, and in the day of manifestation, all things shall appear, even insomuch as they now are present. Wherefore suffer not thyself to be gulled and to be withdrawn from this truth, by such hypocrites who contemning faith, make as if salvation were far from thee, and teach thee in vain to seek it by thy own works. Paul saith, I follow after, if I may apprehend that in which I am apprehended by Christ; that is, that at length I may see the things already given me in the secret bosom of faith. He covets and burns in desire to see that treasure which he hath received through faith already given, but yet shut and sealed up, and afterwards by these and such-like places, whereof thou mayst read not a few in Holy Scripture, where it is testified that we are already saved, and that a believer ought not to seek to attain to Salvation by works, which is that Satanical opinion and doctrine which doth blind the eyes, extinguish the true knowledge of faith and carry us out of the way of truth and salvation. Let us stick to what the Apostle here witnesses, not regarding them that teach as if Salvation were not already given, but must necessarily be attained by other means than Christ alone, which how it sides with the Scripture and the life of a believer, everyone may plainly see, excepting him who hath no insight into the Scriptures. For thus Divine Scripture teach everywhere; and whosoever doth not receive Salvation of mere Grace by faith before all works, that man shall never attain it; and all that refer not their good works to the profit and good of their neighbor, but to their own, being more careful by those works to provide for their own salvation, rather than the good of their neighbors, those have indeed no good works at all, for these men do lack true faith, and are infected with pernicious error."

  Thus far Dr. Luther, between whom and youself, I observe this great difference; that is, that Luther affirmed from plain and express Scripture that a man must first be apprehended by Grace, to lay hold upon heaven, and be truly and really possessed of Salvation, and happiness by faith, before he can do any work that is truly good. But Dr. Taylor teaches that though Salvation be perfected in respect of the causes; yet our faith must hang in suspense, and not actually lay hold on, to enjoy eternal life, until we have spent and ended our life in all manner of good works. In effect, Dr. Taylor saith, that our faith in Christ giveth us only the right and claim to salvation; and when there is an addition of good works too, only then can we become capable of possession. So that we have and enjoy nothing by faith, but only have a right to all upon condition of holy walking. We have not remission of sins, righteousness, favor, peace, salvation, Christ, nor God himself, but are without possession of all these, without God, without

Christ; only our faith puts us in good hope, if we continue to serve and worship God according to his Law, that at our end we shall attain to all. Or if I grossly misconstrue not his meaning, it is this, as I may safely conclude from his words, that a man may be a believer, be justified, be a child of God, have Christ, a member of his body, be united to him, have the unction of his Spirit, be placed and seated together in heavenly places with Christ, and yet shall not be blessed, but upon condition of works; or that a believer hath right to Christ by faith, but he hath not received him yet; or if he have Christ, yet blessedness and salvation be put apart and far separated, not to be reached and touched, unless the hands of faith to be well strengthened, lengthened and cleansed by good works. In brief, faith, saith he, in Justification saves only upon condition of an holy life. What now is become of all infants, dying before they did or could work well? Chrysostom surely then was wide, and those learned and judicious establishers of the doctrine of our Church, who bring him in saying thus, "I can show a man that by faith without works lived, and came to heaven; but without faith never man had life;" unto whom agrees Ambrose, when he declared, "he that believes is saved by faith alone without works;" also Melanchthon, when he stated that, "neither is our obedience either cause or condition of acceptance with God." Dr. Fulke, "this Justification of mere Grace by faith alone without works, is that by which we are saved." Again, Chrysostom, who saith that, "God hath not refused men that have works, but he hath saved them destitute of works, that no man might have whereof to glory." Have not these and innumerable such learned men erred with us in this point or been too hasty and unadvised in their words? Surely if Dr. Taylor might have ruled them, thus they rather should have said that upon condition of good works, faith will save us in the end, and though Justification is free, but Salvation is upon condition of works.

But let us ponder for what end the doctor holdeth this a goodly opinion; secondly, upon what grounds? First, he utterly mistakes that our blessedness, life and salvation should be passive; that any man should take it freely and forthwith as a gift of God through Christ, by faith alone without and before all good works; {which yet is the Apostolic and Protestant doctrine;} but such places of Scripture, as Mark 16:16, "he that believeth and is baptized shall be saved;" and Eph.2:8,9, "for by grace are ye saved through faith; and that not of yourselves; it is the gift of God, not of works, lest any man should boast;" and as Jn.20:31; I Cor.15:2; Tit.3:5, &c., do contain too short a cut to heaven. Paul did carry the jailer too quickly over the gulf of perdition, the broad sea of his sins, God's wrath and destruction, when he promised him simply that he should be saved, if he only believed. Fie on this detestable and erroneous course! Men must be put upon action, at least as necessary conditions before they can be safe. Thus the profound doctor in effect would control and condemn the very wisdom and goodness of God, only in a blind and preposterous zeal of works. Alas Sir, might not this one example, with that of Luke 7:37-47, end the quarrel about this point, rid you of all needless fears, and teach you what a virtuous and powerful thing the true Grace of Christ is, and how well and safely you may trust a believer without his former keeper.

Hence let all men see, that true faith will always work with works, {as it did the faith of Abraham,} and how presently, effectually and freely did these express and declare the truth of faith in the heart. Nowadays men dare put no trust in faith, an argument that true faith is rare. "Nevertheless when the Son of man cometh, shall he find faith on the earth?" {Lk.18:8} But all their evidence and ground for heaven is in their works of reformation and performance; and the proper cause of these is the doctrine of the Law and not of the Gospel. Twigs and forced fruit must be had where it will not naturally and freely grow, and better such than none? Right; but to commend such trees or ground, to persuade or bear such men in hand, that their state and case is good and secure is dangerous and not praiseworthy. True faith is never barren! Well, but to borrow or gather fruit produced by virtue and the urging of the Law, and to appropriate them to faith, as faith will never own such, so it is hypocrisy and not honesty. Thus to deal in civil affairs would be counted mere imposture and deceit, and yet by your religion it is uprightness and truth.

Objection: But are we not commanded to do good works?

Answer: 1. Yes, but not as conditions of life and salvation. True religion teaches that by being children, the inheritance is already ours, and that God doth not cut or cast off his own accepted and adopted sons because of after-undutifullness. "For I am the LORD, I change not; therefore ye sons of Jacob are not consumed." {Mal.3:6} But if we imitate not our Father in love and mercifulness, then we are not what we be taken for; but show ourselves to be bastards and not true sons.

2. The Lord doth not by commanding give either power or disposition to be such, but being first so enlarged and inclined by the doctrine of free Grace, he both wills and ministereth the occasion, that by outward deeds and conversation, we may manifest the same. As if a father bid his child to exhibit and show mercy to a beggar, he doth not thereby make him merciful and compassionate, but by being so before, he would have him declare by relieving of the miserable his inward courteous and pitiful nature,

which he hath alike with his father. Note further the cunning of the doctor; for if one should say, if besides my faith in Christ there be also required good works to Salvation; alas, I am almost never the better or safer for Justification or the Righteousness of Christ. He prevents and instructs him, bidding him seek unto God; for God, saith he, gives the ability to the performance of the same. So {according to this mixed notion} then God enables to be joint saviours with Christ; and if not the cause, yet surely the condition. Again, mark that though God gives the ability to do, yet man doth them, as if he purposed that man should have some hand in saving himself, and were loth that God should have that glory to himself alone. He will have works, the expressions and fruit of sanctification, to be conditions of purpose that man may in some sort share with God in the honor of his own Salvation. How directly is the Apostle against this presumption! Eph.2:7-9. Again, God enables, but man worketh them; then why doth not God work them as well as enable thereunto, lest man should be as a stock and stone? Yet the Scripture testifies that God not only enables, but effectually works the will and the deed. "It is God which worketh in you both to will and to do of his good pleasure." {Phil.2:13} "Make you perfect in every good work to do his will, working in you that which is wellpleasing in his sight, through Jesus Christ; to whom be glory for ever and ever. Amen." {Heb.13:21} And yet man is more than a stone too; for he hath ability to will and work naturally in himself, but that he either willeth or worketh well is exclusively the work of the Lord within him. Your endeavor is too much to steal from God and to pamper that pride of man's spirit which God would have humbled to hell. If you could be contented with the simplicity of the Gospel, then Christ alone and his works, which is not I, and my works of sanctification, will suffice to lead and bring to glory, so that you walk therein by faith. Is not Christ the way, truth and the life? Jn.14:6. Hath he not consecrated a new living way by his flesh? Heb.10:20. Should we know any other way to heaven, to God or true blessedness, or can we walk in and keep this way save only by faith? The just live by faith, and as he receives Christ, so he walks in him by faith. Col.2:6.

But he alleges Matthew 25:35, "for I was an hungred, and ye gave me meat; I was thirsty, and ye gave me drink; I was a stranger, and ye took me in, &c.," bidding us to take heed thereunto, and so that we may not presume of the safety of our standing in Christ, before any such fruit can be seen growing there as he insinuates. How you can make those works of charity conditions of receiving the kingdom, I see not, unless you can show me, where it was promised them upon that condition, but rather I truly see, that the kingdom was by God himself, through his love in Christ Jesus prepared for them from everlasting, so they being found in Christ by faith, having his righteousness, or prepared for it; yea, called, blessed, &c., "Come, ye blessed of my Father, inherit the kingdom prepared for you from the foundation of the world," vs.34. Gal.3:9; Phil.3:9. Secondly, so that good works are there brought on the stage and mentioned to give evidence and testimony of the truth of their justification, which otherwise is invisible and hid from the eyes of the world, and alone is declared unto men thereby, as "show me thy faith by thy works;" as the fruit thereof is not the cause or condition, but only an effect and expression of the goodness of the tree, and so is the case here. And mark how easy a matter it is to beat you with your own weapon; for these works were done simply for Christ's sake, in his destitute members, and not for their own; and secondly, also freely and not as conditions of the kingdom. Yea, thirdly, so far are they from such an intent or thought therein, that they seek to be altogether ignorant or forgetful, that ever they did aim at any such thing. The right hand knoweth not what the left doth. I question not, but if works had been propounded and urged with such importunity, and as conditions so absolutely necessary to attain eternal life, as you teach and press them upon your hearers, then that impression would have remained still, and they in danger of rejection would, pleading their own righteousness as entitlement to the heavenly inheritance. "Many will say to me in that day, Lord, Lord, have we not prophesied in thy name; and in thy name have cast out devils; and in thy name done many wonderful works?" {Mt.7:22}

≡≡≡≡≡≡≡≡≡≡≡≡≡≡≡≡≡≡≡≡≡

Dr. Taylor - Page 73: "This assertion bewrayeth great ignorance of the power and present use of sanctification, and the duties of it; which they conceive as legally urged, to help the believer in his title and right to the blessed inheritance purchased in heaven; whereas only Christ's righteousness and merits, give right and title unto heaven; but yet the grace of sanctification gives us an aptitude and fitness unto it, for without holiness none shall see God, Heb.12:14, and no unclean thing shall enter into the gates of that city, Rev.21:27; yea, it is proceeding in sanctification to the measure and stature of Christ that fits us to the vision and fruition of the glorious presence of God, and for the full possession of the heavenly inheritance."

R. Towne: Indeed it is the great and lamentable ignorance of that one article of Free Justification in Christ, as Dr. Luther saith, that makes you stumble at the Truth; and thus whilst you seek to oppose and suppress it, you misconstrue and pervert almost every Scripture. Secondly, it has been proved that Christ's Righteousness gives both a right and a fitness for heaven, if it be truly put on.

You say, that sanctification gives a fitness for heaven? If our works are the way and conditions of life, and sanctification gives an aptitude, are you note too quick to jump with those, Acts 15:5, who believed and taught the faith of Christ, and yet added, that except they kept the Law, they could not be saved? This is a perverting of the Gospel; and "of the Gospel of Christ, to make it the Gospel of the devil." {Luther} "I marvel that ye are so soon removed from him that called you into the grace of Christ unto another gospel; which is not another; but there be some that trouble you, and would pervert the gospel of Christ." {Gal.1:6,7}

As for the texts, Heb.12:14, without holiness "no man shall see God." What holiness is that, if not of Christ communicated by the Spirit, who shall take of the glories and virtues of Christ, and give it unto you? This is that object of Faith, which looketh on, and enjoys things invisible, Heb.11:1, II Cor.4:18; and by the operation of the Spirit of Faith, it shall be diffused throughout the powers and parts of soul and body like leaven, and after the measure of faith, is sensibly discerned in the light of knowledge, wisdom, peace, joy, patience, confidence, contentment. Secondly, Rev.21:27, necessarily sendeth you to that Fountain "opened to the house of David and to the inhabitants of Jerusalem for sin and for uncleanness" – Zech.13:1; Rev.1:5, and our growing in the unity of faith is the enlightening and enlarging of the heart to a more effectual understanding and full receiving of that immeasurable sea of righteousness, peace, joy, and all manner of blessedness, which is in Christ; that all things may be swallowed up in us thereby, and not a proceeding in legal holiness as you imagine. But grant that grace or the gift of sanctification doth give a fitness, doth it follow that blessedness is not passive? What can you do more towards the sanctifying or changing of yourself than to your justifying? It is God's act to sanctify throughout. "Them that are sanctified by God the Father, and preserved in Jesus Christ, and called." {Jude 1} "By the which will we are sanctified through the offering of the body of Jesus Christ once for all." {Heb.10:10} You cannot make one hair white or black, how then can we in anyway attribute anything to our works? "Can the Ethiopian change his skin, or the leopard his spots? Then may ye also do good, that are accustomed to do evil." {Jer.13:23} Thus the proposition remains clear and sound, being purified and freed from the dust and foulness of your exceptions, aspirations and cavils, which unworthily do deface and obscure it; and now let the reader judge as to who hath swallowed the poison and embraced error.

≡≡≡≡≡≡≡≡≡≡≡≡≡≡≡≡≡≡≡≡≡

Dr. Taylor - Page 74: "That the justified is freed from all spot of sin."

R. Towne: True, imputatively in Christ, but that sin and pollution should not be in the flesh, has ever been denied and rejected.

≡≡≡≡≡≡≡≡≡≡≡≡≡≡≡≡≡≡≡≡≡

Dr. Taylor - Page 74: "Justice requires that God's wrath be pacified."

R. Towne: Wrath is an effect of justice offended by sin; now shall sin remain, and stare in the eyes of justice, and yet there be no danger of indignation? What pacifies God's wrath against sin but the full satisfaction of Divine Justice, and can justice be satisfied until the evil of sin be utterly removed and abolished. "Who being the brightness of his glory, and the express image of his person, and upholding all things by the word of his power, when he had by himself purged our sins, sat down on the right hand of the Majesty on high." {Heb.1:3} "And for this cause he is the Mediator of the new testament, that by means of death, for the redemption of the transgressions that were under the first testament, they which are called might receive the promise of eternal inheritance." {Heb.9:15} "Now once in the end of the world hath he appeared to put away sin by the sacrifice of himself." {Heb.9:26}

≡≡≡≡≡≡≡≡≡≡≡≡≡≡≡≡≡≡≡≡≡

Dr. Taylor - Page 74: "And a righteousness procured whereby the sinner may be accepted in mercy."

R. Towne: Yea, given and applied to the sinner, whereby by the imputation of Christ he is become perfectly pure in the sight of God, Col.1:22, and thereupon accepted in the Beloved; for what favor can we have until we be found first righteous before God without exception?

≡≡≡≡≡≡≡≡≡≡≡≡≡≡≡≡≡≡≡≡≡

Dr. Taylor - Page 74: "But not a plenary and personal perfection."

R. Towne: What is perfection but righteousness? "Seventy weeks are determined upon thy people and upon thy holy city, to finish the transgression, and to make an end of sins, and to make reconciliation for iniquity, and to bring in everlasting righteousness, and to seal up the vision and prophecy, and to anoint the Most Holy." {Dan.9:24} Secondly, is it not plenary when it is complete, Col.2:10, and everlasting? Dan.9:24. Thirdly, and it is personal when it is ours, one with us, put upon, and in us. "For as many of you as have been baptized into Christ have put on Christ." {Gal.3:27} "For he hath made him to be sin for us, who knew no sin; that we might be made the righteousness of God in him." {II Cor.5:21} "In the LORD shall all the seed of Israel be justified, and shall glory." {Is.45:25}

≡≡≡≡≡≡ ≡≡≡≡≡≡≡≡≡≡≡≡≡

Dr. Taylor - Page 74: "They show gross ignorance in the nature of Justification."

R. Towne: I wish heartily that I might cast the mantle of love upon your foul failing in the nature of this chief article of our faith; but the cause is God's, and the least jot or tittle here is of more worth than heaven and earth.

≡≡≡≡≡≡ ≡≡≡≡≡≡≡≡≡≡≡≡≡

Dr. Taylor - Page 74: "Which frees a believer from the condemnation of sin."

R. Towne: True, but first from sin itself, which is the cause, then from condemnation as a necessary and inseparable effect, and consequence of sin by due course of Justice.

≡≡≡≡≡≡ ≡≡≡≡≡≡≡≡≡≡≡≡≡

Dr. Taylor - Page 75: "Thirdly, faith itself in the justified is sincere, but not perfect."

R. Towne: Oh weakness! Is faith any part of a believer's righteousness in the sight of God? Faith is in man, Rom.10:10, and the justified man is perfect in Christ. Col.2:10.

≡≡≡≡≡≡≡≡≡≡≡≡≡≡≡≡≡≡≡≡≡

Dr. Taylor - Page 75: "Now would I know how that which is in itself imperfect, and not free from spot of sin, can make another altogether spotless."

R. Towne: A leprous hand cannot work to get one penny; yet may serve to receive a jewel of inestimable value. If our imperfection of faith hinders the perfection of God's act, then our Justification is imperfect, which is against all truth and the harmony and current of divinity.

# Chapter V

*Dr. Taylor's Fifth Chapter.*

≡≡≡≡≡≡≡≡≡≡≡≡≡≡≡≡≡≡≡≡≡

Dr. Taylor - Page 76: "Containing four more pernicious errors."

R. Towne: Indeed if these be opinions and fancies of man only, they must be vain, and if erroneous it necessarily follows that they be pernicious, but this title imports that they be more than ordinarily dangerous and damnable; so let us read and scan them.

≡≡≡≡≡≡≡≡≡≡≡≡≡≡≡≡≡≡≡≡≡

Dr. Taylor - Page 76: "No action of the believer after Justification is sin."

R. Towne: Surely the doctor is here someway foully mistaken; for no action of a believer or unbeliever, whether before or after justification is sin; for all action hath God for the author in whom all live and move, Acts 17:28; but he cannot be the author of sin, for action is one thing, and the disorder of it is another.

≡≡≡≡≡≡≡≡≡≡≡≡≡≡≡≡≡≡≡≡≡≡≡

Dr. Taylor - Page 76: "For unto faith there is no sin."

R. Towne: What need? For this is no reason to prove the former. Unto faith there is no sin. Is this either pernicious, erroneous or yet strange to you, then what a stranger are you to these Scriptures: "Unto him that loved us, and washed us from our sins in his own blood." {Rev.1:5} "Christ also loved the church, and gave himself for it; that he might sanctify and cleanse it with the washing of water by the word, that he might present it to himself a glorious church, not having spot, or wrinkle, or any such thing; but that it should be holy and without blemish." {Eph.5:25-27} "You, that were sometime alienated and enemies in your mind by wicked works, yet now hath he reconciled in the body of his flesh through death, to present you holy and unblameable and unreproveable in his sight." {Col.1:21-22} "Now unto him that is able to keep you from falling, and to present you faultless before the presence of his glory with exceeding joy." {Jude 24} "And in their mouth was found no guile; for they are without fault before the throne of God." {Rev.14:5} "And such were some of you; but ye are washed, but ye are sanctified, but ye are justified in the name of the Lord Jesus, and by the Spirit of our God." {I Cor.6:11} Faith only fixeth the eye, and heart upon these Divine Testimonies; acknowledging and admitting no other object. It is against the nature of faith to conceive, or to entertain any thoughts of God in relation to herself, which do not in every way suit and agree with the word of faith, which is the Covenant of Free Grace. "Casting down imaginations, and every high thing that exalteth itself against the knowledge of God, and bringing into captivity every thought to the obedience of Christ." {II Cor.10:5} It is the office and special power of faith to captivate and confine every imagination concerning God, as he is alone to be found revealing, and communicating Himself and his mind in the Son of his love, who therefore is called the image of the invisible God. Col.1:15. God will be known to faith none otherwise than in Christ; and so it's a fancy or fiction to imagine a universal, non-illuminated, and confused faith in God, which can never bring into acquaintance with the true God.

In brief, {though both plenty of matter in the great weight and necessity of the argument do call and excite to a more full enlargement,} as nothing ought to be propounded to faith but the doctrine of mere Grace, {for the Law is not of faith, Gal.3:12,} so that doctrine, if it be pure, testifies assuredly that Christ hath washed, Rev.1:5, hath purged, Heb.1:3, and abolished, Heb.9:26, all our sins, and hath made us holy, unblameable and unreproveable in the sight of God. If that thus by the beams of the Sun of Righteousness, Mal.4:2, all the sins arising out of these earthly members of our flesh continually be dispelled and consumed forever appearing between God and us, like as darkness and mist is at the presence of the sun; and faith only casts up and directs her eyes to these ample and clear heavens of Grace, and never looks aside to consider what may be found re-pungent to this record and work of Christ, either in ourselves or in any other creature; how then can it be, but that all must be clean and pure to faith? "Unto the pure all things are pure; but unto them that are defiled and unbelieving is nothing pure; but even their mind and conscience is defiled." {Tit.1:15}

What a cloud of orthodox and approved writers, who have held and recorded the same might be here produced; but since Luther is sanctioned in your midst, let him speak, for thus he writes, "so mightily worketh this grace of faith, that he that believeth that Christ hath taken away his sins from him, is like Christ void of sin;" and upon Galatians 3:13, these are his words, "faith layeth hold on this innocence and this victory of Christ. Look therefore how much thou believest this, so much doest thou enjoy it; if thou believe sin, death and the curse to be abolished, they are abolished; for Christ hath overcome, and have taken these away in himself, and will have us to believe, that like as in his own person there is now no sin, nor death; even so there is none in ours, &c. There is no defect in the thing itself, but in our skepticism; for as to our reason, it is a hard matter to believe these inestimable good things and unspeakable riches. Moreover, Satan with his fiery darts and his ministers with their wicked and false doctrine go about to wrest this truth from us, and utterly to deface this holy doctrine, and especially for this article, which we so diligently teach, we sustain the cruel hatred and cruel persecution of Satan and the world. For Satan feeleth the power and fruit of this article; and that there is no more sin, death or malediction since Christ now reigneth, we daily confess in the Creed of the Apostles, when we say that we believe that there is a holy Church, which is indeed nothing else but I believe, that there is no sin, no malediction, no death in the Church of Christ. For they that believe in Christ are no sinners, &c." Read on for your further satisfaction. And if even either you or any other, have heard us, {whom you rate and call at your pleasure,} to have taught or held otherwise, then let us be accountable for it. Is now Luther yours or ours? If you condemn us, why not him, unless you love to be partial?

≡≡≡≡≡≡≡≡≡≡≡≡≡≡≡≡≡≡≡≡

Dr. Taylor - Page 76: "It is out of the element of the Law to judge of this blessed condition."

R. Towne: True, for the law is not of faith, Gal.3:12, and it is the part of the Gospel to blot out the handwriting; and to erase out of our minds that opinion and sentence of the Law which is natural; and to write or imprint another opinion and knowledge of God. But this cannot be effected without great conflict, and wrestling of our mind and spirits. For our natural conscience strengthened by the Law is ever reclaiming and contradicting what the Gospel testifieth. Only the word of faith can truly discern and judge of this matter of faith. For where does the Law speak a syllable of our conjunction in union with Christ, whereby Christ and the believer become one body in spirits. "For we are members of his body, of his flesh, and of his bones." {Eph.5:30}

≡≡≡≡≡≡≡≡≡≡≡≡≡≡≡≡≡≡≡≡

Dr. Taylor - Page 76: "Neither can God allow any work that is defective in the believer."

R. Towne: True, for perfection is the ground of acceptance both of our persons and performances; as imperfection or sin is the cause of rejection or loathing. How strongly and truly you confute these, we are now to consider in their order.

≡≡≡≡≡≡≡≡≡≡≡≡≡≡≡≡≡≡≡≡≡≡

Dr. Taylor - Page 76: "Here is the ghost of H.N. in this piece of new Gospel, which tells us a dream of an absolute reign of faith, where is still remaining sin. True it is that faith deposes the reign of sin that it rule not, but so as that it itself never reigns in this life without the presence and assault of sin; for, such as say they have no sin with their faith, deceive themselves."

R. Towne: Here is the ghost of H.N., and may we not say that Paul hath well foretold us what great skill you have in these things, I Cor.2:11-14, wipe your eyes and guess again what spirit either we or you are of.
    A dream, you say, of an absolute reign of faith. A flat mistake; for if you look again the truth tells you that by the blood of Christ sin is so taken away that none remaineth in the kingdom where faith reigneth through righteousness, and sits as judge. Faith, you say, deposes the reign of sin that it rule not; but you pervert the state of the question, the better to decline the edge of the truth; for a fair fall from Justification to inherent sanctification; from the doctrine of Christ in faith, to law and works.

≡≡≡≡≡≡≡≡≡≡≡≡≡≡≡≡≡≡≡≡≡≡

Dr. Taylor - Page 77: "It is enough for the state of this life, that faith frame the heart to a willing and sincere obedience, though not to perfect and absolute obedience."

R. Towne: If, as you say, faith frame the heart, then the Law frames it not; and though this obedience be not perfect as it proceeds from us, yet Justification is that salt that salteth every man, and every sacrifice that it may be acceptable. "For every one shall be salted with fire, and every sacrifice shall be salted with salt." {Mk.9:49}

═══════════════════════

Dr. Taylor - Page 77: "It argues their gross ignorance in the Scriptures, which affirm that both persons, and duties of believers, though imperfect and defective are yet pleasing. For their persons God looketh upon them in Christ, and pronounces of them, that though they be black, yet they are comely. Ps.147:11. Secondly, for their duties, they yet please him, because their persons do; and our comfort and happiness is, that he pleases to accept from us that which is sincere, though weak and imperfect."

R. Towne: Gross ignorance! Though you must be suffered to speak, yet your words be but wind, and your Scriptures will not say as you would have them. All that can be gathered from them is, that God doth allow and accept of such a people, and of their service; but the ground or cause of acceptance of the one or the other, is not once mentioned, unless you will expound them after this manner. "The LORD taketh pleasure in them that fear him, in those that hope in his mercy;" {Ps.147:11;} to wit, because they fear him, which sense I should think you intended, if it were not too far gross for so learned and judicious a divine. That the Lord taketh pleasure both in the persons and duties of his elect, is granted on both sides; but herein we differ; for you say, {but prove not,} that the halt, the blemished and defective find acceptance; but we affirm the contrary. What a crack and flourish you make to deceive simple minds, when as in solidity of argument, or truth of matter, you cannot produce one syllable against us; but something must be done to gratify the lookers on. You have given them our assertions here, four in number, under such titles and epithets as might more fitly have been reserved for such as deserved them far better. I hope that the first three do now look fair and comely, being cleared from your aspirations, the fourth is made good thus; that whatsoever is not perfectly and completely righteous is not accepted of God. Imperfect works are not perfectly and completely righteous; therefore, imperfect works are not accepted of God. The assumption or minor cannot be denied; and all the question is about the major proposition, which is yet verified. Gal.3:10; Hab.1:13; Rom.1:18. Whence I thus argue.

What God hath manifested to be detestable and accursed, that he cannot accept. But he hath manifested by Holy Scripture, that whatever is not absolutely perfect, is detestable and accursed. Whatsoever is not absolutely perfect, cannot be accepted with God. The proposition is grounded upon the constant virtue and immutableness of God, who cannot deny Himself, or recall his word, and with whom is no variableness nor shadow of change. James 1:17 God will not suffer the loss of the least tittle of His righteous Law, Mt.5:18, nor alter any part of His unchangeable will. In the one whereof He most strictly and indispensably requireth without all possibility of mitigation, abatement or favor, that everyone present himself, and all his works absolutely entire and perfect, according to the exact and spiritual meaning of his whole Law; and by the other he is necessarily, naturally, and immutably inclined and bent to love or hate, to accept or reject, to bless or curse; everyone without respect of persons, as he shall be found just or unjust. Psalm 5:4,5.

If it be said, that there is infinite mercy with the Lord; it is answered, that even mercy saves not, but by due course and order of Divine

Justice; as it receives none into favor without perfect satisfaction out of the Law.

If it be replied, that God looketh upon all in Christ, and so is well pleased with all. I answer; it is true, that God regardeth and accepteth both the persons and the works of believers in his Son; but yet not as they are in themselves impure and defective; but as they are changed, washed, purified, and made thoroughly perfect in that clear and all healing fountain of His precious blood, and everlasting righteousness. "In that day there shall be a fountain opened to the house of David and to the inhabitants of Jerusalem for sin and for uncleanness." {Zech.13:1} "Come now, and let us reason together, saith the LORD; though your sins be as scarlet, they shall be as white as snow; though they be red like crimson, they shall be as wool." {Is.1:18} Thus Abel and his sacrifice through this glorious tincture and dye put upon it by the merits of Christ, were accepted. Heb.11:4.

If it yet should be condemned or contemned by any, because it's commonly taught otherwise, or because it's but the judgment or opinion of some new novices, I will a little labor to remove this stumbling block from before thy feet also; yet shortly and orderly.

1. Where there is not perfect righteousness, there undoubtedly is the curse of God.

2. Obedience is neither cause nor condition, for which we are accepted of God.

3. Our debt was a great deal too great for us to have paid, and without payment God the Father would never be at one with us; therefore it pleased him {Christ} therefore to be the payer thereof, and so to discharge us quite. Everyone knows, {if it were not as a price in the hand of a fool,} that the debt that we owe is to be perfectly and constantly throughout all the passages of our

life, answerably to the exact requirements of the Law of God.

4. The Law perpetually without any moderation or abatement of its full rigor, denounces that condemnatory sentence that cursed is everyone that continueth not in all things written in the Law to do them, Gal.3:10; who now is able to stand and abide in this so terrible presence of the just God, that is, destitute of a perfect righteousness, which is nothing less than the satisfaction of the whole Law.

5. Whilst a man is suffered to stand to his own judgment, he imagines that to be righteous is mere hypocrisy, wherewith contenting himself by I know not what stained justice, he opposes the free Grace of God; but after he is forced to examine his life by the balance of the Law, he no longer presumes upon that feigned righteousness, seeing how immeasurably short he is of true holiness, and how he abounds with infinite vises, of which he thought himself clear before; for the evils of concupiscence are so deeply and secretly hid, that they soon deceive man's outright.

6. For this end is the Law given, that of great it may make little; that it might show how thou hast no ability to attain righteousness of thyself, that so as a poor worthless and beggarly wretch, thou mayest hasten to Free and Sovereign Grace.

7. God holds us all at the staves end, to humble us, testifying that all by nature are utterly lost and damned, as the rest of Adam's line. 2. That there is no soundness, nothing but corruption and abomination in us, and in our ways; thus it stands us upon, that God justifies us by his own mere and alone goodness, and looks upon us singly in Christ, and that we only rest in his promise. Let us leave all things that men imagine to bring themselves into favor with

God, by mingling this and that with faith, for they are all but falsehoods and illusions of Satan.

8. And why are we justified? Because God cannot love sinners until he hath forgiven their sins, and put them quite away. We know that forasmuch as God is righteous, he cannot agree with sin, but must needs always hate it. Then, since the case stands so, if we intend to have his favor, we must needs first be cleansed of our sins; for so long as they come into reckoning, God must needs hate and curse us; but contrariwise, when the LORD wipes away all our sins, then receives he us in mercy, and by that means do we begin to be blessed of him. We are discharged of our sins, as of a debt paid, &c., by means whereof our sins are quite wiped out, for as they come not anymore to account or remembrance before God, and therefore we are justified and blessed in Christ.

Again, to the intent he may be no more an enemy, and take part against us which are sinners, he must be pleased to look upon our Lord Jesus Christ, and upon his righteousness, the same may do away all our offenses.

Have not all these godly and learned men held and taught the same, that we do at this day; namely, that Justification by Grace alone in Christ Jesus doth bring us into the well pleased and everlasting favor of God, II Cor.5:18-19, and that this Justification consists of these two parts; that all our sins must be utterly wiped and done away, so as they never come up into remembrance with God, through the merits of Christ's blood. Secondly, that in the Righteousness of Christ, we must be made perfectly and everlastingly righteous. "For he hath made him to be sin for us, who knew no sin; that we might be made the righteousness of God in him." {II Cor.5:21} "For as by one man's disobedience many were made sinners, so by the obedience of one shall many be made righteous."

{Rom.5:19} Thus the justice of God in his holy Law, terribly threatens and accurses us, shuts us out of God's presence, denies us all access or hope of favor and acceptance, till we come through faith in Christ Jesus to be made holy, unblameable and unreproveable in his sight. Col.1:22. Must we not then of necessity be perfect; yea, complete in Christ, that we may be accepted. "For in him dwelleth all the fulness of the Godhead bodily. And ye are complete in him, which is the head of all principality and power." {Col.2:9-10} "That the righteousness of the law might be fulfilled in us, who walk not after the flesh, but after the Spirit." {Rom.8:4}

But some have objected, that our persons are perfectly holy and righteous through the free donation and communication of Christ's merits and righteousness, but not our works. This arises from the ignorance of the nature and extent of free Justification, which being but the application of this sovereign salve, the blood and obedience of Christ, so as that was but once made sufficiently and perfect, to cure all by Christ himself. "For by one offering he hath perfected forever them that are sanctified." {Heb.10:14} So is it by the Spirit, and by faith in the ministration of the word, but once given and received to heal all sins and infirmities, throughout the whole course of our life. The justified live always by faith in this, and so are ever sound and safe. This one sentence is certain and immutable, that the Righteousness of Christ availeth forever with God for all our sins, wherewith being once justified, they are always so, and need not their own righteousness to pacify God for sin, &c. God's mercy by Jesus Christ does not cause him to put off, deny or any way to abate any part of this justice; which it should do if God did not reward or regard any person, or duty, as it is defective or imperfect. True, our best works as done by us are imperfect, but before they can come up into the presence and acceptance with God, they necessarily must be salted, purified from their corruption and filthiness. The incense was to burn between God and his people to perfume their unsavory breath, and to make their prayers an odor of a sweet smell, otherwise their pollution and defect is such that rather they are to be judged for sins than virtues.

Let Calvin be consulted with, {Institutes, book 3, chapter 17, section 8-10,} and he will make good against all gainsayers, what you reprove and condemn. He telleth you that those good works which follow Justification are esteemed and valued otherwise than after their own desert and dignity, because whatever is imperfect in them is covered with Christ's perfection; whatever blemish or filthiness is cleansed by his purity, lest it should come into question by God's judgment. Therefore the fault {note, he saith not guilt and punishment} of all transgressions being blotted out, whereby men are hindered from bringing forth anything acceptable to God; also the defect or imperfection which is wont to pollute all good works being buried, all good works of the faithful are acknowledged to be just, or which is all one, are esteemed as righteous in Christ. Read of the next section for better satisfaction, where he saith, that otherwise the works of the faithful would be impure, unclean, done by halves, unworthy the sight of God, much less worthy of his love or delight; and is it not now obvious to every eye, that Calvin holds perfection both of the person and performance in Christ, to be the ground of acceptance with God. To deny this is to deprive God of the purity of his holy nature and pure justice, which cannot look upon or take pleasure in any impure or sinful thing. "The foolish shall not stand in thy sight; thou hatest all workers of iniquity." {Ps.5:5} Secondly, to deny that Christ's blood and righteousness truly and effectually applied, hath wrought any cure or soundness in anything. "All we like sheep have gone astray; we have turned every one to his own way; and the LORD hath laid on him the iniquity of us all." {Is.53:6} "For he hath made him to be sin for us, who knew no sin; that we might be made the righteousness of God in him." {II Cor.5:21} "For as by one man's disobedience many were made sinners, so by the obedience of one shall many be made righteous." {Rom.5:19} And it is against the office of Christ's Mediatorship and Intercession, whilst our own supposed worthiness in our works must speak and plead for acceptation. I Pet.2:5. Fourthly and lastly, it presumes that Christ hath, if not abrogated, yet I know not how mollified and tempered the attribute of Divine Justice, rather than to have fully satisfied and contented the same. And why should Paul call and account his own righteousness as dung, which is of such esteem with God? Phil.3:8. God looks upon them, you say, in Christ; yea only, and always doth God behold his Church in that innocence and righteousness, in which Christ rose from death to life, and pronounces of them, say you, that though they be black, yet are they comely. Christ pronounces and affirms of her, no otherwise than as his Church in his eyes, being clothed with the robe of Christ's purity and holiness. "I will greatly rejoice in the LORD, my soul shall be joyful in my God; for he hath clothed me with the garments of salvation, he hath covered me with the robe of righteousness, as a bridegroom decketh himself with ornaments, and as a bride adorneth herself with her jewels." {Is.61:10} In herself indeed, in the glass of the Law, reason, and sense, she appears black; but in Christ through the Gospel, she was beautiful and comely to the eye of faith.

Calvin in brief answers all your other Scriptures, saying, that they declare rather who they are that God taketh pleasure in, then the ground and cause why, which he plainly and plentifully affirms to be the alone perfection which is communicated by Jesus Christ. You too little perceive the danger of placing the confidence of acceptance in our own inherent dignity or worthiness of works, whilst thus without cause you pick quarrel against us. Our comfort, you say, and happiness is, that he pleaseth to accept from us that which is sincere, though weak and imperfect. Nay our comfort and happiness is, that whereas God in justice can accept of nothing that is imperfect, he hath made our works and persons perfectly holy and good, that so He may accept and delight in them both. "And lo a voice from heaven, saying, this is my beloved Son, in whom I am well pleased." {Mt.3:17}

≡≡≡≡≡≡≡≡≡≡≡≡≡≡≡≡≡≡≡≡

Dr. Taylor - Page 78: "That our preachers teach Popery, in persuading good works to further men's own Salvation."

R. Towne: Our preachers? Have you any which we have not? If thus craftily you would intimate any separation, let it be then of yourself, and your confederates from the Truth of Scripture, and of the established doctrine of our Church, and from us, with, and in the same, for I am sure hitherto none appeareth to be made by us. For their teaching of Popery let others judge, I Jn.4:1, for who ever teaches or approves this your book is not far from it, whatever he say or profess otherwise. Tit.1:16. To further men's own Salvation? If you would clear yourself of this accusation, you should {as hath been sufficiently proved before} persuade to good works, because we are freely justified already, and saved without works; yea before all works. "Not by works of righteousness which we have done, but according to his mercy he saved us, by the washing of regeneration, and renewing of the Holy Ghost; which he shed on us abundantly through Jesus Christ our Saviour; that being justified by his grace, we should be made heirs according to the hope of eternal life." {Tit.3:5-7}

===================================

Dr. Taylor - Page 84: "The sum of his answer to the third error is this; to clear it, we teach that a good work must arise from a good worker. We teach duties necessary to Salvation, not as causes or merits, but as a way of ruling; and so the Apostle preached them necessary. "Let ours also learn to maintain good works for necessary uses, that they be not unfruitful." {Tit.3:14} We distinguish between the justice of works which conduces not to Salvation, and the presence of works without which there is no Salvation, but all faith is dead, and religion vain. James 2:26. We distinguish between the principal efficient and the instrumental causes, as the gospel, faith, ministers. "For in doing this thou shalt both save thyself, and them that hear thee." {I Tim.4:16} What will you say to Paul who commands us to work out our Salvation with fear and trembling, Phil.2:12, or to the Apostle who calleth duties a furthering our reckoning, Phil.4:17, and a sowing, "he which soweth bountifully shall reap also bountifully," II Cor.9:6; who saith that Christian sufferings turn to the salvation of the saints, II Cor.1:7, that they cause unto us an eternal weight of glory, II Cor.4:17; and to Peter, who saith, that by an addition of graces, an entrance is ministered abundantly into the kingdom of Christ, II Pet.1:11; if we may not urge the doctrine of good works and Christian duties in pretense of the Law's abolition?"

R. Towne: To clear it, you make a harsh and offensive crackling, and a hollow sound of fruitless words, by which you darken the knowledge of free Justification by only grace in Christ, and thereby offend the minds of the simple. If there be any word bearing weight against our tenent, we shall consider it, and others let pass as idle and to no purpose.

Not as causes, you say, but as a way. If Salvation be in Christ already perfectly and everlastingly accomplished; tell us if there be any other way or means to come to Christ than Grace alone, by faith alone. Eph.2:8-9. God's workmanship "created in Christ Jesus unto good works" as the way of the kingdom; and not the way to the kingdom, as you do, as if the believer were out of it, or short of the kingdom. "For the kingdom of God is not meat and drink; but righteousness, and peace, and joy in the Holy Ghost." {Rom.14:17} If I be one hundred miles from London, my way thither is one way, but the way of London in which you walk who are citizens, or live, abide and dwell there is quite another.

As impertinent and helpless is that also of Titus 3:14, to your purpose. "And let ours also learn to maintain good works for necessary uses, that they be not unfruitful." Are there no other necessary uses, nor ends of good works than Salvation or Justification, then they are not necessary at all, for that is dispatched before they come. Besides the margin in the last translation will tell you, that it might be well rendered thus, "let ours learn to profess honest trades for necessary uses;" trades are necessary and useful. Therefore will you turn tradesmen that you may be saved. All that you can reap when you have labored to weariness, is that saving faith is not without good works; but that it saves not therefore without them, either as joint causes or conditions, is no good nor direct consequence.

You say that you distinguish between the justice of works, and the presence of works, without which there is no Salvation. It salvation and life be the next and immediate consequent fruit of justification, so that no sooner can a man be justified, but forthwith he is saved in the same instant, Rom.5:18; Jn.3:36, then their presence will not be suffered in this point, or, {yet we will not grant, since God allows us not} if Justification do work before it saves, will you against the consent of all Orthodox writers in this deny that faith comes singly and alone adorned, beautified and dignified with Christ's Righteousness, and unaccompanied with our works into God's presence to obtain Salvation at his hand; or if God see the Righteousness of the Son of his love, will not this sufficiently move him to accept and save, unless he find an addition and presence of our works, which in the best are so defective, beggarly and filthy, that without Justification they deserve rejection and condemnation. The stars give a goodly and useful light in the night, but at the rising and presence of the sun they are wholly obscured, and their splendor is utterly lost. So is it with all good works; {which though they be highly esteemed and profitable amongst men;} yea, even the best and most sincere, if they come into the presence of God, will die out in an instance. Bernard knew it to be the safest to respect and mention the righteousness of God, Christ, or of faith alone, saying, "what shall I sing of my own righteousness of works; nay Lord, I will make mention of thy Righteousness only, for that truly is mine, since Christ is of God made to me Righteousness." Luther, {whom you say to be yours,} saith, "when we reason of righteousness, life and everlasting salvation, the law and works must be removed out of sight." Also he that gave you, I think, that distinction would have told you, that works are necessarily present in the justified, because the justified in Christ, are also sanctified by the Spirit, but not as a cause or joint cause efficient deserving or furthering salvation, but as a necessary benefit annexed to Justification as a fruit of faith. If their presence be in the justified, will you say, therefore in the point of Justification and Salvation? Then you have both many, and the truth against you.

Fourthly, you say that you distinguish between the principal efficient and instrumental causes of justification. To what end is all this? Christ alone hath saved us, the word only testifieth it, the ministers expound that word, faith wrought by that heavenly ministration through the operation of the Spirit alone goeth to Christ, apprehends him to salvation, unaccompanied of works. Thus truly taught the apostles, and all that ever went with a right foot to the Gospel of Christ. The question is of works and you argue for faith, and the means thereof.

Fifthly, you ask what we will say to Paul, &c., I say that you have here heaped together the choice Scriptures, and arguments of the Papists, as if you intended publicly to testify what you are, and with whom you side, and how resolved you are to derogate what you can from faith, grace, Christ, and God; and to transcribe it to man and his dunghill works. You envy that Christ's righteousness should have all the reward and glory. And therefore the holy men of God shall speak what they never intended to patronize your sinfully undertaken quarrel. Paul, you say commands to work out our salvation; and the same Apostle testifieth elsewhere, that our salvation is already finished by Christ alone, and that God hath saved us, and called us with an holy calling, not according to our works. II Tim.2:9. Shall Paul now be at odds and disagreement with himself, rather than you will grant salvation to be before works, or to be attained without condition of works? For thus is your mind prepared and set well. How then is Scripture to be reconciled? For salvation is but one, and in essence imperceptible; though Christ hath saved His people, yet is this treasure hid, till God reveal his Son in us, Gal.1:16, and make known the unsearchable treasures of his grace in Him by the Gospel, through the Spirit of Illumination and Faith. Hence we are called upon to work it out, which is carefully to attend upon the ministry of this reconciliation, which sheweth us where our Righteousness and Life is, Job 36:3, and so convinces, persuades and unites the heart unto it; yea and because our sight and strength spiritual as well as natural of the body admits of degrees, we are exhorted daily to edify ourselves in our holy faith, to grow up in the knowledge and grace of our Lord Jesus Christ; yet all this is but diligence in the means of breeding and nourishing faith, which is the only necessary work to compass and lay hold of Salvation.

Yea and whilst both pastor and people be thus diligent in the means, whatever good is wrought thereby is only ascribed to God. He worketh both the will and the deed, we do what is in the power and reach of nature; but whatever is spiritual, and any whit available to apprehend Salvation that God worketh in us. We at the best work but passively, and are therefore bid withal to work with fear and trembling; that is, with much dejectedness and diffidence of ourselves, to wont ourselves alone to look up unto the power of God which worketh all in all. Or, the Philippians are commanded to continue working and walking in the faith received, until the day of the sensible manifestation and fruition of their Salvation, and not to be removed by any enterprise from the hope of the Gospel. Is this to make Salvation defective till works have made it out? This implies no more but the necessity of believing, or diligence in the means of revealing and applying of Salvation which is perfectly accomplished by Christ alone, lest we should be found the neglecters of so great Salvation. Heb.2:3. But what maketh this to be the clearing of, or will you unwarrantably conclude from this place that you might persuade people to good works to further their Salvation? Surely the works of faith are only needful to Justification and Salvation, and works for our conversation before men.

In reference to Phil.4:17, "not because I desire a gift; but I desire fruit that may abound to your account;" I answer that your reckoning must be according to your works of faith, which reckoning is furthered, when your works {done freely without respect to either reward or condition of Salvation thereby} do show and witness to the world how true, simple and effectual your faith in Christ's Righteousness alone was in your inner or hidden man of the heart. As the works and miracles that Christ did when his Divinity was questioned did further, that is, clear, evidence and put it all out of question and doubt.

But here you say, that "mercy accepts that for a furthering of our reckoning, which in strict justice would not go for payment." It's too true, that by this resolute opposing of the evident Truth of God, you have brought yourself into that labyrinth and straight that you cannot reconcile your own tenents, otherwise than by setting the lovely and never jarring attributes of God at complete variance. Now mercy is brought to accept what in justice {without abatement} she may not. What rocks do you unhappily and indiscreetly dash your ship against? I have both said and proved that mercy doth not save or accept us of our works with the least prejudice or dispensation of justice. Also it is foul and intolerable; yea, it's that arrogant presumption which antichrist sets up against Christ, to affirm that man's works are joined with Christ's in the work of Salvation, or that mercy taketh us into that work. For answer, I like neither, but profess myself an adversary to both; yet I must needs be the one, for I had much rather be an Antinomian than an antichrist professor; for I shall no longer wonder that the doctrine of free Grace is so contradicted and blasphemed everywhere; now that I see such profound madness against it.

Again, whereas you muddy that Scripture, II Cor.9:6, "he which soweth sparingly shall reap also sparingly; and he which soweth bountifully shall reap also bountifully;" I answer that we shall reap the honor and credit of what in true love to Christ {because he hath procured eternal life and blessedness freely and alone for us} we do to any of the saints, whilst whatever we have done or suffered for their benefit shall be revealed and published in the last day before men and angels. Thus, who so honors Christ shall be honored by him. Who so confesses him on earth, &c., "whosoever therefore shall confess me before men, him will I confess also before my Father which is in heaven," {Mt.10:32;} "whosoever therefore shall be ashamed of me and of my words in this adulterous and sinful generation; of him also shall the Son of man be ashamed," {Mk.8:38;} "this I pray, that your love may abound yet more and more in knowledge and in all judgment; that ye may approve things that are excellent; that ye may be sincere and without offence till the day of Christ." {Phil.1:9-10} Faith alone inclines and enables to do and suffer all for Christ; so that alone is rewarded and regarded, for God respected his Son and his Righteousness alone, which, as is proved to be extended and communicated to all the passages of our life, so it alone giveth the dignity of acceptation, otherwise our works of themselves be unworthy in the sight of God. "But without faith it is impossible to please him; for he that cometh to God must believe that he is, and that he is a rewarder of them that diligently seek him." {Heb.11:6}

That passage in II Pet.1:11, is also by you objected, where the Apostle saith, "for so an entrance shall be ministered unto you abundantly into the everlasting kingdom of our Lord and Saviour Jesus Christ." As faith is effectual in producing such fruits, so answerable it establishes, quiets and comforts the conscience, yet is but an argument from the effect to the cause. You say, "as runners by speed and strength get nearer their goal;" but if they run thus from Christ to themselves, from the righteousness of faith to works, they do but run out of the way. The true Christian gets near the goal; that is, the full revelation and sensible fruition of that Salvation he possesses already in Christ, whilst he goes on from faith to faith. Rom.1:17. See yet how you pervert the apostles and slander us if we debar any from urging good works aright, or either pretended or intended the abolition of the Law, which certainly will prove to be injured and abolished far more by yourselves than any of us.

≡≡≡≡≡≡≡≡≡≡≡≡≡≡≡≡≡≡≡≡

Dr. Taylor - Page 87: "They deny all outward worship since Christ's coming, by Jn.4:23; yea, and inward also, excepting faith; and they say also, that there is no reward to any good work; but good works have their reward; Pv.19:17, Mt.10:42, Rev.22:12, and in keeping the commandments there is great reward."

R. Towne: Surely, here is a double mistake; of the exposition, and of the inference and rash sensor grounded upon it. First, the believer by faith performs all both the outward and inward worship required in the Law, "that the righteousness of the law might be fulfilled in us, who walk not after the flesh, but after the Spirit," Rom.8:4, and is a true fulfiller of the Law. Perhaps some have been misinterpreted, {a usual thing in your disciples, who can neither skill to retain, nor repeat rightly almost any point of true faith,} when they have said that it is the only work required in the New Testament, because it contains and includes all in it. So that our love and confidence towards God, fear, patience, humility, &c., doth all arise and spring from this grace of faith. Hence, preach Christ, and you preach all. "Whilst I bid a man believe, I bid him do all things," saith learned Robert Rollock on John; and then how wide you are in so false a consequence as you make, every one may see; as if you knew not the doctrine, nature and power of Justification.

Works, you say, have their reward. We shall find works extolled to the heavens, the reward is reckoned to the worker being in Christ of mere Grace by the faithfulness of the Promisor, I take it that you grant, first, that the Covenant of Grace must be first laid as the foundation of all favor and felicity; secondly, through the obedience of Christ as the effect of that Covenant, the procurer and deserver of all favor and respect is both communicated to the believer and his works, to give them all cause of acceptance with God; also it hath all the promise of good things solely appropriated and annexed to it. So that where Christ's Righteousness is, there is both regard and reward, but not for any worth or value in works, which without Justification are foul and loathsome, and as dung, Phil.3:8, and deserve to be cast out of God's sight and presence. Now what is this in the issue, but that Christ is the only pearl of great price which is honored and recompensed by God in all our ways; or that Justification is the parent or cause of all blessedness. "So then they which be of faith are blessed with faithful Abraham." {Gal.3:9} Paul bids us, I Cor.15:58, to "be ye stedfast, unmoveable, always abounding in the work of the Lord, forasmuch as ye know that your labour is not in vain in the Lord;" that is, seeing the resurrection is certain, and you know the crown, honor and felicity due through Christ's Righteousness will far more than compensate, bring in and restore whatever is either dispensed by your charity or lost by affliction for Christ and his Gospel sake.

≡≡≡≡≡≡≡≡≡≡≡≡≡≡≡≡≡≡≡≡≡

Dr. Taylor - Page 88: "That God sees no sin in the justified; for he seeth no iniquities in Jacob. Num.23:21."

R. Towne: Be it far from me to question what I know to be by justice duly scanned, censored and punished; yet seeing you have linked and conjoined all the supposed errors that do most often offend you, and endangered as you think your hearers in one system or body; so that he that defends some, must needs speak for, or to all, or else a worst imputation will be charged upon him, let me entreat the consideration of these few queries, which methinks do much tend to pacification and unity. The phrase is God's, and he is happy that can in any way be helpful to pick out the true sense thereof. "He hath not beheld iniquity in Jacob, neither hath he seen perverseness in Israel." {Num.23:21}
 1. First, I would demand whether God be propounded in the Scripture, to be known or considered of us according to his simple nature or being, as he is an incomprehensible Majesty or according to the manner of revealing and communicating of himself?
 2. Secondly, whether we are to know anything of the mind of God in reference to us,

and our condition before him, save as we find the same mentioned in the two covenants, Law and Gospel.

    3. Whether we see sin, be not an act simply of that Divine Justice, which is attributed to God in reference to his Law, and is not affirmed of his simple essence? It is true that God knoweth all actions and things, "for in him we live, move and have our being;" but to see either person or action sinful and unclean, must needs be with respect and eye to a Law; for sin is a transgression of the Law.

    4. Whether in the mediation of atonement, Christ our Surety had all our sins laid upon him, and appropriated to him, Is.53:6, Ps.38:4, and so did stand in the presence of Divine Justice, as the only malefactor and sinner of the world, being by imputation truly clothed and charged with all our sins?

    5. And appearing under this form, as a public person, whether the Divine Justice of the Law did not rightly acknowledge him to be the transgressor and debtor, and so made him to suffer whatsoever was the desert of those whom he represented. For first the Lord made to meet on him the iniquity of us all, Isa.53:6, and then delivered him to be put to death. "Who was delivered for our offences, and was raised again for our justification." {Rom.4:25}

    6. Are not the principle clear and divested in the face in court of Divine Justice, whose debts are translated from them to their Surety, and completely satisfied for by him; so that it is truly said that they are blameless, and as such can be accused of no crime in God's sight. "In the body of his flesh through death, to present you holy and unblameable and unreproveable in his sight." {Col.1:22} "Who shall lay anything to the charge of God's elect? It is God that justifieth." {Rom.8:33}

7. I can look upon myself, my actions, yea, into my conscience, and see my sins remain; but look into the Records of Heaven, and God's Justice, and since the bloodshed of Christ, I can find there nothing against me, but that the bond of my Surety has satisfied and canceled; and even these present sins which so fearfully stare in my face, are there blotted out of God's book of remembrance. "For I will be merciful to their unrighteousness, and their sins and their iniquities will I remember no more." {Heb.8:12} And as a debt discharged has become a nullity with the Lord. Faith seeth an everlasting expiation, which causeth shame and fear to flee away; and therefore my peace and happiness consists in the forsaking, and not considering of myself, and in my living and abiding in Christ, who is in heaven, where is perfect purity and cleansing forever. And this is to live, and walk by faith, and not by sight.

8. Whether a Christian, a justified man, who hath reference to Christ alone, being united to Him, made one with Him, and by the imputation of His obedience, is become the righteousness of God, and so is a certain spiritual person, a son of God, heir of the world, conqueror of the world, of sin, death, and the devil &c., and who only can spiritually be discerned by faith, ought to be considered in relation to the Law of works, and to be judged by reason and sense, according to his outward condition and life among men? For thus to fall from justification to inherent sanctification, from faith to works, is to pervert the state of the question. And whilst you thus consider him, as he is in himself apart from Christ, and according to the Law and to works, he then ceaseth to be justified to your thoughts, and is brought from heaven to earth, and is found to be a sinner, accursed, and condemned, and one in whom God and men see sin. These queries are pertinent to

the point in controversy, and may happily give some light to the right understanding of it. What contentment another may reap by your books I know not, but I profess {save that your mind and scope is to oppose} that I find little either solid, distinct or punctual; neither can I tell where to have you, yet it will be expected I say somewhat to your arguments.

≡≡≡≡≡≡≡≡≡≡≡≡≡≡≡≡≡≡≡≡≡≡

Dr. Taylor - Page 88: "There is a simple eye and knowledge of God, whereby he cannot but see all things."

R. Towne: What God in his simple nature or essential understanding knoweth, or how he seeth is further above our comprehension than the heaven is above our heads. "For my thoughts are not your thoughts, neither are your ways my ways, saith the LORD. For as the heavens are higher than the earth, so are my ways higher than your ways, and my thoughts than your thoughts." {Is.55:8-9} But if {as you here do} you will make sin to be the object of this incomprehensible sight, I see not but it will follow that sin must then be co-eternal with the essence of God and coexist eternally in the mind of God without beginning or end, which however it will be true in respect of the general ideas or notions of all things, existing in the Divine mind from eternity, yet in respect of particular instances, and of the manner of the actual existence of things in the world, I conceive that the Lord is said to know them after another different manner; also it cannot but be in accord with the essence of God to know his creatures distinctly and particularly, and to know the nature and qualities of man, or the world, &c., for God might have existed, though none of these had ever been, being absolute and all sufficient in himself;

neither did the knowledge of things arise from the absolute necessity of his nature, but from the free liberty of his will, moving {though eternally} his understanding to his actual knowledge of the creatures.

And although the knowledge of God whereby he knoweth himself and the patterns of all things he intended from eternity to create; and that knowledge whereby he sees everything as it is now existent, and brought into act here on earth, be one and the same in God; yet the Scripture will both warrant and teach us to consider the diversity thereof; to wit, one way as it subsists in the mind of God, foreseeing and appointing all things; and another way as it is actuated or brought into act, having relation to things now extant before our eyes, about which it is always conversant. For as the manner of existence of the designs or patterns of all things God purposed to make {which were from everlasting in the mind of God} differeth from the manner of their existence now being made; or, as the existence of all things which God before the creation, may be distinguished from the existence or instance given them by actual creation, so doth the knowing of them differ also. Then they were known as purposed to be created; now as actually made and fashioned every way according to that pattern of his eternal counsel and good pleasure. Then he knew them as being and existing with himself, and in himself; now as they are produced to actual existence and public view. Then God saw what he intended to make, but after the creation, it is said, that the Lord saw all things that he had made, Gen.1:31; and thus though God seeth no new thing, yet he seeth them after a new manner. And if the creature change, as, it is by the will and finger of God; so he doth see the change, and the condition into which it is changed. But I leave this transcendent and curious subject to be disputed by those who are endued with the knowledge of the holy, Pv.30:3, and to be determined when they can; for well I know it is far too high for me, this knowledge of God being like himself incomprehensible. And by a more exact inquisition into it, I may come to be confounded by the exceeding glory of such majesty. Only this, I say, that your argument is wide indeed, while it leads to a consideration of all things, as they stand in relation to God's sight or knowledge without any succession, time or change, whereby a coeternity and unchangeableness of being and condition before the eyes of God, must necessarily be granted to everything, though itself be never so mutable and momentary. Thus God by one simple, individual and immutable act seeth Adam before he made him, and after his creation, in his innocence, fall and redemption by Christ, as he is miserable and blessed, as he is in part holy by inherent sanctification, and as he is perfect and glorified in Christ. In all these stations, &c., states that Adam had waded and passed through he still remained before God, with whom nothing is transient. Thus God seeth his Son incarnate, crucified and dead, as well risen, and seated at his right hand in glory; and thus he as well and alike seeth his elect in the first Adam, polluted, miserable and accursed; and as in Christ, washed, justified and blessed. Yea, if the LORD still sees sin in the saints in heaven, &c., why then is the question so stated, whether God sees sin in the justified? God seeth sin in the elect, as he seeth them impure and unjust before faith; but he seeth them pure from all spot of sin as they be washed in the blood of Christ and justified in his Righteousness.

You say, that he cannot but see all things, and it is true that God doth see every work and distinguish between the action and the evil thereof, though you do not.

≡≡≡≡≡≡≡≡≡≡≡≡≡≡≡≡≡≡≡≡≡

Dr. Taylor - Page 92: "What God directs to a certain end, he must needs see and know."

R. Towne: I have not read before that God directs or orders sin, or hath any hand in it, as sin. So far as any action or motion is caused, guided or disposed by God, so far is it pure and good, and so is the effect and end thereof. Besides, sin is no positive thing ordered by God, but is a defect, a disorder in the actions of men, over-ruled and disposed of in accordance with Infinite Purity and Divine Wisdom.

≡≡≡≡≡≡≡≡≡≡≡≡≡≡≡≡≡≡≡≡≡

Dr. Taylor - Page 93: "One attribute of God destroys not another, his mercy must not destroy his wisdom."

R. Towne: God's wisdom hath found out such a way for the purging and abolishing of sin utterly by Christ from the eye of his Justice, that now mercy may justly save, not to the least impeachment, but to the full praise of Divine wisdom, justice and mercy.

≡≡≡≡≡≡≡≡≡≡≡≡≡≡≡≡≡≡≡≡≡

Dr. Taylor - Page 93: "What God makes them see in themselves, himself must necessarily see."

R. Towne: If this argument hold, then God must confess and bewail sin, as well as see sin; for you say that he makes the believer to do all these. But the truth is that God's mind and pleasure is, that after effectual calling the believer should alone cast his eyes on Christ; abide in him, and his Righteousness; rejoice continually in this so full, complete and blessed condition which God hath freely advanced him unto; and so let the confession of the tongue both arise from and agree with this faith and confidence of the heart, and not return unto bondage again. "For with the heart man believeth unto righteousness; and with the mouth confession is made unto salvation." {Rom.10:10} "We having the same spirit of faith, according as it is written, I believed, and therefore have I spoken; we also believe, and therefore speak." {II Cor.4:13} "For ye have not received the spirit of bondage again to fear; but ye have received the Spirit of adoption, whereby we cry, Abba, Father." {Rom.8:15} As faith looks directly and exclusively to Christ, so it is the nature and force of reason, sense and infidelity to eye and consider what is in me, and elsewhere out of Christ, and his Gospel. Rom.4:19; Heb.11:11.

Besides you reason along the same lines. The Law and Gospel passeth over the heart of every believer daily; their voices, operations, and sentences are contrary. The conflict in the conscience thereby causeth more grief, and unrest, then ever did Jacob and Esau in Rebeckah's womb; and it will ever continue until the one be destroyed and extinct. Faith and Infidelity do strive within me, about me, to whether of them I should appertain. And now I yield to the Law, and infidelity, and say and confess with bitter lamentation that I am taken captive, &c., anon faith, and Christ appears, and reviseth, recalling, erecting and enlarging my spirits, and putting in my heart and tongue a new song of praise, victory and salvation to my God and King, because He hath redeemed, justified and saved me. In all the examples of the saints, it is one thing what they should, and another often what they do. David prayed that his sins might be pardoned, which you grant were pardoned. Now did he thus pray according to the truth and confession of faith, and the effectual apprehension of forgiveness?

≡≡≡≡≡≡ ≡≡≡≡≡≡≡≡≡≡≡≡

Dr. Taylor - Page 95: "He that records the sins of the elect many years and ages after they are pardoned, sees sin in the justified."

R. Towne: You stray, and come not once near the mark which you shoot at. See your reasoning in the like. God records that the waters did once cover the face of the earth in the creation, and afterwards in the days of Noah, therefore he sees them so now? He hath recorded that Joseph was in prison, Israel in Egypt, Daniel in the lions den, therefore he seeth them there still? It is recorded also that Christ hath loved us, and washed us from our sins in his own blood, Rev.1:5, why then doth not God behold us washed?

≡≡≡≡≡≡ ≡≡≡≡≡≡≡≡≡≡≡≡

Dr. Taylor - Page 96: "Objection, but these were in the Old Testament; so was the death of Christ less efficacious to them than us?"

R. Towne: Christ and his benefits were the same in the Old Testament as they are in the New Testament, but yet the ministration much differed. Then God hid and veiled the Son of Righteousness, under the thick and dark cloud of the Law, in the constant ministry whereof, as a choice instrument for that purpose, he showed himself to be exactor of their righteousness of works for life and peace; to be a diligent observer of their manners, a narrow searcher and severe punisher of all sin and iniquities. Thus God dealt with them rather as a hard lord with his servants according to their ways than as a Father of mercy, a Justifier, and Saviour by Christ. They were sons in truth of adoption, but in education and condition differed not from servants. "Now I say, that the heir, as long as he is a child, differeth nothing from a servant, though he be lord of all; but is under tutors and governors until the time appointed of the father. Even so we, when we were children, were in bondage under the elements of the world; but when the fulness of the time was come, God sent forth his Son, made of a woman, made under the law, to redeem them that were under the law, that we might receive the adoption of sons." {Gal.4:1-5}

≡≡≡≡≡≡≡≡≡≡≡≡≡≡≡≡≡≡≡≡≡

Dr. Taylor - Page 98: "Do they never read the Scriptures wherein so many believers sins are recorded, which yet were many ages before pardoned? I Cor.6:11; Rom.6:19; Eph.2:11; Col.3:7. But let them hide themselves in their own thickets, to enjoy more securely all their licentious courses."

R. Towne: As all these examples be of the same size and sort with the seventh section, so the answer there given may well suit and serve them. To let pass your scornful and reproachful words; yet I may not {gentle reader} forget or neglect to admonish thee of this one thing more, to wit, that the Doctor takes it for granted, that if it be received and yielded, that God seeth not {in his gross sense} the sins of the justified, then is a wide gate opened to all Libertinism, and the justified then may and will enjoy securely all licentious courses. May not any man perceive by this what little acquaintance and experience he hath of the true nature, office and operation of Free Justification; and that all his best works be but eye-service, like that of an unfaithful slave. Eph.6:6. And in a word, as one wittily said, how he loveth and serveth God wickedly. For faith and Christ in the Gospel have no power with him in the soul freely, sweetly and willingly to incline, and enlarge it both to love, and to the duties of love commanded; but the overlooking eye and the terror of the Law of God are needed and these keep him within compass. This is his due commendations, his practice triumphs with his doctrine, and both are in opposition to Christ and true Christian liberty.

# Chapter VI

*Dr. Taylor's Sixth Chapter.*

═══════════════════════════

Dr. Taylor - Page 98: Dr. Taylor charges us with this error, "that God is not displeased with the sins of the justified."

R. Towne: It is strange that you should give credit to such a report. Could ever any harbor such a senseless opinion, that fire and water, light and darkness, life and death, righteousness and sin could ever be agreed? The righteousness of God doth so necessarily, naturally, and immutably incline and move him, to hate and curse sin, in whomsoever, that the LORD spared not to pour such a sea of wrath and vengeance upon that only Son of His love, when he stood before him charged with the sins of others. Can any think that God can be less displeased with sin in his adopted sons, which is also of their own committing, than he was with it on his only begotten Son, when it was only his by imputation? Or that Christ by his cross should destroy that enmity which was between sin and righteousness, and not rather abolish sin utterly, the sole cause of hatred, and variance between God and his elect, and so to make peace. "But now in Christ Jesus ye who sometimes were far off are made nigh by the blood of Christ. For he is our peace, who hath made both one, and hath broken down the middle wall of partition between us; having abolished in his flesh the enmity, even the law of commandments contained in ordinances; for to make in himself of twain one new man, so making peace." {Eph.2:13-15} But I think there is some mistake here, an easy and usual thing among these kinds of professors, who have little skill to concede or retain any sound tenent of the Gospel, their eyes being so veiled, and their hearts so leavened with the Doctrine of the Pharisees. Thus perhaps it should have been delivered, that though the justified do sin continually, for in many things we sin all, James 3:2, yet God is not displeased nor angry with them; the ground of which seemeth to be this, that Christ remaineth forever a Mediator between God and His Church, Heb.12:24, speaking perpetually Peace by virtue of his blood, thereby banishing, and keeping away continually all the evils and failings of his peculiar from the sight and presence of his Father; and by means of his everlasting righteousness, Dan.9:24, the virtue and preciousness whereof infinitely exceedeth the evil of all sin, and doth preserve God and his people in perpetual unity, communion and love. Rom.5:1. "Wherefore he is able also to save them to the uttermost that come unto God by him, seeing he ever liveth to make intercession for them." {Heb.7:25} If we sin, we have an Advocate, Christ is the propitiation for our sins. Christ doth not reconcile us to God, and then leave us in danger of procuring God's displeasure by our after failings and backslidings. No, the Scripture witnesseth an inviolable Covenant of peace and a life forever established in the death of the Testator; so that it is of free and pure grace without our dependency and conditions of our works or worth. The ground of our exception against that is that you consider the nature of sin, and of God's justice, not regarding the atonement for sin, the virtue whereof extends universally to all sins, and times.

≡≡≡≡≡≡≡≡≡≡≡≡≡≡≡≡≡≡≡≡≡

Dr. Taylor - Page 99: "They conceive not that anger and love may be at the same time tempered in a father to his children, whom because he loveth he chasteneth."

T. Towne: Yes, we conceive and grant, that in the sense of Scripture, anger and love may be at the same time in God towards his children, and so allow of your distinction, provided that it be referred to the state of the Church before Christ's resurrection; but we see yet no reason or ground, why we may or ought to admit of the application of it to the New Testament, unless you hold this a necessary and fit consequence. The child is tutored and nurtured, put the school and whipped for his faults in his childhood, therefore he is so when he is come to the estate of a man, and is permitted to be at his own choice and liberty. Gal.4:1-2.

     But you object, {pg.102,} "hath Christ done less for believers in the Old Testament than in the New? I answer, Christ is the same yesterday and today and forever." The virtue and efficacy of that one offering of himself once for all is alike diffused and extended to all ages, but the administration is different. Christ's purchase is the same for all his elect, but it is not in a like manner and measure dispensed to all in this militant condition. Paul's similitude best sets forth his own meaning. The love of a father is as great and tender to his son in his minority, as when he is full-grown, and the heir in his non-age is as truly lord over all in respect of right; but yet hath not actual, free and full possession until the time appointed; and so believers in the Old Testament had the adoption, or were as truly adopted as believers be now, but they had not the spirit and immunities of the sonship. "For ye have not received the spirit of bondage again to fear; but ye have received the Spirit of adoption, whereby we cry, Abba, Father; the Spirit itself beareth witness with our spirit, that we are the children of God." {Rom.8:15-16} Now though God was indeed to them a Father, yet whilst he veiled and concealed this his paternity and graciousness from them by the ministration and strict exaction of the Law of works under severe penalties, and manifested himself in another relation, namely, of a schoolmaster to his scholars, or as a tutor to his pupils, or as a lord to his servants, whose office and part it is to correct and rebuke all inordinate walking; may it not rightly be said that both they displeased God, and that he made them to suffer for their offenses, yet in a way of correction only, and not of satisfaction? The Scripture and approved authors are very clear and full in setting forth this difference of condition and government, however you with others have little observed the same. This may serve to minister occasion at least of more diligent search hereafter. Consider well these Scriptures: Acts 15:10; II Cor.3:6; Heb.7:19; 9:9; 9:24; 11:13; Gal.3:23; Mal.4:2. "For ye are not come unto the mount that might be touched, and that burned with fire, nor unto blackness, and darkness, and tempest, and the sound of a trumpet, and the voice of words; which voice they that heard intreated that the word should not be spoken to them anymore; {for they could not endure that which was commanded, and if so much as a beast touch the mountain, it shall be stoned, or thrust through with a dart; and so terrible was the sight, that Moses said, I exceedingly fear and quake;} but ye are come unto mount Zion, and unto the city of the living God, the heavenly Jerusalem, and to an innumerable company of angels, to the general assembly and church of the firstborn, which are written in heaven, and to God the Judge of all, and to the spirits of just men made perfect, and to Jesus the Mediator of the New Covenant, and to the blood of sprinkling, that speaketh better things than that of Abel." {Heb.12:18-24}

"Neither, say you, doth this wrath rebound and seize upon their persons, but sins." Indeed I confess my ignorance and unacquaintedness with this phrase, and always deemed that chastisements, though for their faults had ever been inflicted upon their persons. How wrath should seize upon their sins and their persons escape, I understand not? Sure I am that offenders did ever cry, that they felt the smart of God's anger and rod, yea, and the child will tell you, that he is corrected for his offense.

You call us confused men, but as confused as we are, before we knew you we could distinguish between persons and sins, and say that God did ever so hate evil both in the elect and reprobate, loving his own work and hating that of the devils, which is sin. For even those yet in unbelief are not positively enemies of God, otherwise than their sins are hateful to his justice, and therefore, he saith, "as I live, saith the Lord GOD, I have no pleasure in the death of the wicked; but that the wicked turn from his way and live; turn ye, turn ye from your evil ways; for why will ye die, O house of Israel?" {Eze.33:11}

Dr. Taylor - Page 100: "Christ hath not borne all our punishment of correction, for we must daily bear his cross, and fulfill the remainders of the sufferings of Christ."

R. Towne: Strange doctrine and new, that what we suffer deservedly as evildoers, should be called the cross of Christ, and the corrections for faults counted the fulfilling the remainder of the sufferings of Christ. See I Pet.2:10; 3:17,18; 4:15,16. It is evident, that to suffer as an evildoer for his offenses, is opposed to the suffering as a Christian. Do you not see yourself to be rash and confused, even where serious consideration is requisite, and where you pretend to use most exact distinguishing? Make you no difference between the sufferings for Christ, and the sufferings for sin; between suffering for righteousness, and as an evildoer? Or whereas Christ for our sins endured the punishment of malediction, must he daily now in His members be afflicted with the punishment of correction for sin, even so often as they are hated, reviled, and evil entreated of the world. For so Calvin expounds that place, Col.1:24, of the sufferings which Christ suffered in His members, in which God in his secret and everlasting counsel hath appointed to the mystical body, that is, to the Church of Christ.

Indeed; either you or I mistake the nature of reconciliation; for I simply take it to be an agreement and friendship between two which were at odds and variance, which could not be effected by our Mediator, save by the expiation and abolition of sin, the seed and cause of enmity. "Now in Christ Jesus ye who sometimes were far off are made nigh by the blood of Christ. For he is our peace, who hath made both one, and hath broken down the middle wall of partition between us; having abolished in his flesh the enmity, even the law of commandments contained in ordinances; for to make in himself of twain one new man, so making peace." {Eph.2:13-15} "And you, that were sometime alienated and enemies in your mind by wicked works, yet now hath he reconciled, in the body of his flesh through death, to present you holy and unblameable and unreproveable in his sight." {Col.1:21-22} Yea and by bringing in Everlasting Righteousness, the elder sister to Peace. "Seventy weeks are determined upon thy people and upon thy holy city, to finish the transgression, and to make an end of sins, and to make reconciliation for iniquity, and to bring in everlasting righteousness, and to seal up the vision and prophecy, and to anoint the most Holy." {Dan.9:24} "Neither by the blood of goats and calves, but by his own blood he entered in once into the holy place, having obtained eternal redemption for us." {Heb.9:12} Thus as reconciliation rightly understood, implies first a freedom from sin {passively and imputatively} so it necessarily infers a freedom from correction for sin. Isa.53:5. You object, Heb.12:6; as the LORD "scourgeth every son whom He receiveth &c." I answer, the Apostle saith not that they are chastened for sin, but if they were without chastisement, &c. Surely your self-confidence and mistaken concept of us, make you Goliath-like thus rashly to rush upon us to your own hazard. We have felt the dint of this weapon before it came to your handling, and thus it hath been answered.

  1. That there is a great difference between the Justification of a whole Church, and of particular persons in that Church; for a whole Church is not justified absolutely, but only respectively, that is, is so reputed in respect of the true believers within it; and so consequently it will not hold, that because a Church collectively is reproved and corrected, {it consisting of divers sorts of people,} therefore that every person in

that Church is reproved. A husbandman complains that his cornfield is all tares and weeds, and yet he sees and acknowledges some good and fruitful ears of corn. So Revelation chapter 3, &c. Such as are baptized into Christ, and have put on Christ by a true faith, are without reproof, "holy and unblameable and unreproveable in his sight," Col.1:22, and are much commended. "Thou hast a few names even in Sardis which have not defiled their garments; and they shall walk with me in white, for they are worthy." {Rev.3:4}

2. In a mixed assembly some belong to the election of Grace, who being summoned and called to come in, do for a time but dally and trifle with the Gospel, therefore they must feel the sharp rebukes and lashes of the legal schoolmaster for their folly, to compel them to come in, Lk.14:23, and to drive them to Christ. Gal.3:23-25. Now these are under the whip, because they be not yet acquainted with their Justification by Christ.

3. It is granted that afflictions as all outward things befall alike to the just and unjust; but yet the Scripture mentions only these three causes, why the godly are afflicted in the days of the Gospel.

First: To try their faith, whether they will abide constantly in the truth of this testimony, that Christ hath slain and abolished all enmity, and made everlasting peace between God and them, even now in the appearing to sense and reason to the contrary. "My brethren, count it all joy when ye fall into divers temptations; knowing this, that the trying of your faith worketh patience." {Jas.1:2-3} "Wherein ye greatly rejoice, though now for a season, if need be, ye are in heaviness through manifold temptations; that the trial of your faith, being much more precious than of gold that perisheth, though it be tried with fire, might be found unto praise and honour and glory at the appearing of Jesus Christ." {I Pet.1:6-7}

Secondly: To conform and make them like Christ in suffering. "And if children, then heirs; heirs of God, and joint-heirs with Christ; if so be that we suffer with him, that we may be also glorified together. For I reckon that the sufferings of this present time are not worthy to be compared with the glory which shall be revealed in us." {Rom.8:17-18} "Beloved, think it not strange concerning the fiery trial which is to try you, as though some strange thing happened unto you; but rejoice, inasmuch as ye are partakers of Christ's sufferings; that, when his glory shall be revealed, ye may be glad also with exceeding joy." {I Pet.4:12-13}

Thirdly: To quicken and increase faith, causing them in these sharp storms of crosses more diligently and firmly to keep and gird closely this perfect garment of Christ's Righteousness, of which end it seemeth that place, Heb.12:10,11, is meant, "for they verily for a few days chastened us after their own pleasure; but he for our profit, that we might be partakers of his holiness. Now no chastening for the present seemeth to be joyous, but grievous; nevertheless afterward it yieldeth the peaceable fruit of righteousness unto them which are exercised thereby." So that in some sort and sense, here respect seems to be had to sin, not principally, but secondarily and occasionally, not as it offendeth God {who by that One sacrifice is forever pacified, Heb.10:14, Mt.3:17,} but as it offends or troubles the minds of the faithful. Not that afflictions simply, properly, and immediately do ease, cure, or quiet the conscience {for their natural fruit and affect, is to deject and terrify like the Law, of which they are appendices,} but that they awaken, and stir up our dullness and security to a more lively, effectual, and enlarged apprehension of Christ and His Righteousness, the only procurer of health, peace, and rest. "Come unto me, all ye that labour and are heavy laden, and I will give you rest." {Mt.11:28} In time of danger, the coney hasteneth to the Rock, the hare to the thicket, the Egyptians to their houses, Ex.9:20; the faithful to the Name of the Lord {the Lord our Righteousness, Jer.23:6,} as their strong Tower of defense. "The name of the LORD is a strong tower; the righteous runneth into it, and is safe." {Prov.18:10} And thus whilst God useth afflictions as a tender father the rod, the cause hath not properly with him the nature of sin, which is an offense to Divine Justice; but it is now considered as a disease troubling his child, which in love, and much pity he seeks to make riddance of in a manner aforesaid, and not in anger and displeasure as you would. And thus the text also saith, "whom He loveth he chasteneth," Heb.12:5; and so therefore I wonder to see you so transported, as to affirm that those afflictions are merited by sin, and are from Justice, which cannot punish the guiltless; and to that purpose to bring that place, Gen.18:25, as if whatever sin deserved, had not been afflicted upon Christ, who suffered the Just for the unjust. "For Christ also hath once suffered for sins, the just for the unjust, that he might bring us to God." {I Pet.3:18} Does, or can sin merit any more than death? Gen.2:17, Rom.6:23. And hath not Christ tasted and undergone the same? Heb.2:14. And is not Justice forever fully satisfied? "Who shall lay anything to the charge of God's elect? It is God that justifieth." {Rom.8:33}

  Or lastly, are the justified still guilty before the Justice of God? You outshoot all your confederates that I know; for they grant that Christ hath freed us from the guilt of sin, and the punishment. And how well serveth that Scripture, Gen.18:25, for your purpose; for by this the justified should be again spoiled and robbed of the everlasting garment of Christ's Righteousness, and of their peace thereby, passing all understanding, and indeed be set again in the same condition and condemnation of the wicked and unjustified. Thus you play fast and loose with your hearers.

"Or satisfy {say you} for sins past." Answer: How past, what before Christ suffered, and who or what satisfies for sins committed since his passion? Or secondly, past, that is, done before we believe in Christ, and what purges and satisfies after conversion? I hope your monitory castigation is no satisfaction to justice, nor that you will not always be of that mind, that weeping and mourning, and tears of repentance can purge sin and satisfy wrath. Can you ever free yourself from Popery, or from gross ignorance of the everlasting efficacy of Christ's blood, and of the nature, extent and effect of free Justification, or from being opposite to true and pure Grace?

Again, we object {say you} that there is no place in the New Testament to show believers corrected for sin, yet you prove it yourself by, I Cor.11:30, "for this cause many are weak and sickly among you, and many sleep, &c." The answer to Heb.12:15-17, &c., may serve here also, but for what cause was it, for eating and drinking unworthily, I Cor.11:27, and doth a justified person eat and drink unworthily? The very beginning and least measure of true grace; of unworthy before, now maketh worthy; and why may it not be said that these Corinthians so chastened for unworthy receiving, did but dally with the Gospel, and did not truly and actually put on Christ and his Righteousness? You say, because it is added, vs.32, "but when we are judged, we are chastened of the Lord, that we should not be condemned with the world;" but they that must not be condemned with the world, are not carnal and hypocrites; yes, till they believe and be washed in the blood of Christ they be no otherwise than carnal, but God doth therefore sharply rebuke and correct his chosen, to drive and fasten them to the Laver of his Son's blood and righteousness, that so they may through Christ alone escape damnation. "Verily, verily, I say unto you, he that heareth my word, and believeth on him that sent me, hath everlasting life, and shall not come into condemnation; but is passed from death unto life." {Jn.5:24}

Then, you object, it's enough that Christ reigns to maintain our peace, by weakening and subduing the power of sin daily. Answer: It is not enough, nay rather it is none of Christ's reign for the maintaining of our peace properly, which here you mention; for Christ reign is in giving and preserving peace by free Justification alone. "Therefore being justified, by faith we have peace with God through our Lord Jesus Christ." {Rom.5:1} "That as sin hath reigned unto death, even so might grace reign through righteousness unto eternal life by Jesus Christ our Lord." {Rom.5:21} And secondly, the effect of this is the abating of the power of sin in the flesh. You dream that his scepter is the Law of works, but truly it is the doctrine of Faith and Grace alone.

≡ ≡ ≡ ≡ ≡ ≡ ≡ ≡ ≡ ≡ ≡ ≡ ≡ ≡ ≡ ≡ ≡ ≡ ≡ ≡ ≡

Dr. Taylor - Page 108: "That the justified have no more to do with Repentance."

R. Towne: If repentance be rightly understood for mortification, confession of sin, or the forsaking of ourselves {as it ought to be;} I say that it is impossible that it should be separated from faith, being ever a companion of it, both in regard of the person justified, and of the time of working; for how can a man be prepared, or have way to faith, but by confession, I Jn.1:9; or how can a man be said to go to Christ, but necessarily there must be a renouncing of himself, Phil.3:8; or how can a man put on the white and precious garment of Christ, but he must needs cast and put off his own filthy and beggarly raiment of his own works? How can a man live and grow in Christ, but he must die and decay in himself? Surely, the believer liveth in a continual denial of himself, abhorring of his own ways; but this is not the whole, no the choice and chief of the day's work is behind, namely, to believe in the Lord Jesus. Hereby gets a believer all his life, peace, consolation, and blessedness; to repent is to condemn all our works, righteousness, and judgment, and the best things in us; and then by faith to flee to free grace. It's said, "repent and believe the gospel," Mk.1:15; that is, distrust and forsake your own righteousness, and embrace Christ in the promise. I see that you can make your house clean daily by tears and humiliation without Christ and his blood, and I cannot but think that it is because some condemned your mistake of repentance, and attributing too much to it, and therefore you conclude, that they deny the use of true Repentance.

≡≡≡≡≡≡≡≡≡≡≡≡≡≡≡≡≡≡≡≡≡

Dr. Taylor - Page 112: "No believer is to pray for the pardon of sin."

R. Towne: This is a consequence of your own, or of some of your faction; for I have often heard it made by such dolts, as would needs conclude a fight and opposition between the creeds, teaching to believe the forgiveness of sin, and the Lord's prayer, and teaching to pray for forgiveness daily; but though it be a common thing with justiciaries and hypocrites, out of blindness or malice, to make such absurd and false conclusions from the evident and undeniable Truth of God, {as Rom.3:5-8,} yet if they had one spark of common honesty in them, they might father and own their own brood and brats.

===============================

Dr. Taylor - Page 117: "That preachers ought not to preach the Law to believers."

R. Towne: I have often heard divers complain, that they did barely hear either the Law or Gospel purely and rightly taught, according to II Cor.3:7-9, and that they should rejoice in the true and sound preaching of either, and therefore I must think that this is but a false accusation and slander against the ninth commandment; for I never yet knew any that was not willing and glad to hear the doctrine of the Law, so that sure it's not the right and distinct handling and use of it, but your corrupt abuse and perverting of it, which is distasteful; but how gladly you take this occasion of insulting and triumphing over us, and the truth in us, who are esteemed base and contemptible vessels. II Cor.4:7. Let the reader judge, and more than a vain flourish and needless repetition of what is both urged and answered formally, I find not.

    Only to section 5, I say, that to him that diligently observes the drift of Christ in the exact exposition and powerful application of the Law, and in the peremptory requiring of a righteousness, exceeding the righteousness of the Scribes and Pharisees, it will appear by destroying and raising that ground of all confidence, and rejoicing in man's works, he seeks to make way and place for the bringing in and establishing of the Righteousness of faith; and for this you may be toppled with authority and commentaries. However your sanctification, which you do so stand and plead for, bred and caused by your legal teaching and motives, doth not exceed Paul's before his conversion to the Faith in anything that I can discern.

≡≡≡≡≡≡≡≡≡≡≡≡≡≡≡≡≡≡≡≡≡

Dr. Taylor - Page 121: "No man can teach the obedience of faith, but therein he must teach the obedience of the Law also."

R. Towne: Here you love to cast a mist before the simple. In the Law of Moses, if a man died without issue, his brother or kinsmen was to marry his widow, and raise up children unto him, which should be called after the first husband's name, yet who begat them? So there is none {whatever your ill will undertakes to the contrary} that denied good works to be necessarily done, which are the fruits that the Law, our former husband should, but never could, {it being weak through the flesh, Rom.8:3,} produce in us; but now the Law and the conscience being parted by death, {for the Law reigns unto death and condemnation, Rom.7:10,} and by grace being united and married to Christ, do by him bring forth fruit unto God, even perfect obedience imputatively, and simple and sincere holiness through the operation of his Spirit, received by the ministry and doctrine of faith, and not of the Law. "For the law was given by Moses, but grace and truth came by Jesus Christ." {Jn.1:17} "How shall not the ministration of the Spirit be rather glorious?" {II Cor.3:8} "This only would I learn of you, received ye the Spirit by the works of the law, or by the hearing of faith?" {Gal.3:2} These fruits are called the obedience of the Law, and the justified are called perfect keepers of the Law, which name he hath only by faith in Christ, and love the effect of faith, Gal.5:6, and this is the fulfilling of the Law. Rom.13:8. But what is caused and accomplished by Christ simply and exclusively by himself, being learned and received by the doctrine of the Gospel, must that be sought and labored for by the ministry and urging of the Law. For this is the main question between you and us; and I dare appeal to the conscience of your simple and honest hearers, that either all, or the most common and usual power communicated by your preaching to their consciences, for the bringing forth of fruits worthy amendment of life, is by your constant teaching, zealous pressing and fearful threatenings of the Law, Gal.3:12; so that what performances you obtain at their hands, cannot be said to be by the operation of the Spirit and faith, unless you will say that the Law is of faith. Aptly and truly saith the doctrine of our Church, "whether thou wilt or no, that work that cometh not of faith is naught. Where the grace of Christ is not the foundation, there is no good work what building soever we make; there is one work in which be all good works, that is faith which works by love, if thou hast it, thou hast the foundation of all good works."

≡≡≡≡≡≡≡≡≡≡≡≡≡≡≡≡≡≡≡≡≡≡≡≡

Dr. Taylor - Page 122: "How false and absurd is it to say, that preachers teaching obedience to the Law of God, teach men thereby to hang upon their own righteousness, &c."

R. Towne: When you promise acceptance and speak peace to your people upon the terms that they endeavor to reform and conform according to the Law, and teach that the conscience of their sincere and holy walking must give them boldness and confidence towards God; and that it doth infallibly testify the truth of their conversion, and that they are in a state of grace, {when most know not what grace is,} and that the favor of God may be regained by tears of repentance, loathing and avoiding of evil, and promises to amend, &c., and lastly, when you teach them to appear before God, to plead and deal with Him in their own righteousness; what do you else {yourselves being judges,} then cause men to hang upon their own righteousness, thereby to stand or fall, to be accepted or rejected, and so you establish a judicial righteousness, being far from the Evangelical Righteousness both of justification and sanctification, and then it's neither false nor absurd to charge you with this. But I wonder that you blush not to papistically to slander us, as of those good works which arise from a true and lively faith, for the joy of favor and blessedness already obtained by Christ to declare the truth of conversion, to glorify God, &., were our great eye sore, when as your own heart in your bosom will sufficiently acquit us.

===========================

Dr. Taylor - Page 124: "Thus having set down these twelve articles of libertine and antinomian faith."

R. Towne: Thus you have run yourself out of breath, I am sure, for I found you far out of the way both of truth and charity; yet you have the world in hand, as there are as many more behind in your study or memory, which more easily you can barter with than justly charge us with them, as I see by your instances, which whoso owns may contend with you.

===========================

Dr. Taylor - Page 124: "In fine, you forbear, as you say, many things."

R. Towne: And if you had once thought that by giving this just occasion of laying open and publishing the truth, that you should have so discovered your own nakedness and infirmity, you would have forborne this pain both in pulpit and press. Doubtless the truth is so loose by you, that only the wings of your own fame are scorched by the light and power thereof.

≡≡≡≡≡≡ ≡≡≡≡≡≡≡≡≡≡≡≡≡

Dr. Taylor - Page 127: "Here is a generation of men swelled up with pride."

R. Towne: Is your tongue your own? Ps.12:3. Whilst you would plead for the Law, will you become lawless? Did ever we hold of attaining a full perfection of sanctification in this life? You know even the spirit in your own bosom, and in your disciples, that it is an untruth and base slander. Oh, the loftiness of your pride and passion! How are you transported with what unjustly you condemn in us? The cynic with a pretended humbleness and modesty of mind would trample Plato's magnificence, but it was easy to observe that he sought to do it out of great arrogance and contempt. Good reader, thou must suffer me to pass lightly over, if not altogether untouch, what I find personal, for my intent is only to clear and maintain the doctrine of true Justification, which is, as Luther said well, heavenly, though we in our conversation and works be earthly.

≡≡≡≡≡≡ ≡≡≡≡≡≡≡≡≡≡≡≡≡

Dr. Taylor - Page 130: "Let it be considered, wherein the Scripture places the perfection of saints."

R. Towne: You utterly err and mistake, for doth not the Scripture place perfection in justification, and define it to be an entire and absolute estate.

"And ye are complete in him." {Col.2:10} "But of him are ye in Christ Jesus, who of God is made unto us wisdom, and righteousness, and sanctification, and redemption." {I Cor.1:30} "For by one offering he hath perfected forever them that are sanctified." {Heb.10:14} Doth not justification imply an expiation and abolition of sin? "Unto him that loved us, and washed us from our sins in his own blood." {Rev.1:5} "But ye are washed, but ye are sanctified, but ye are justified in the name of the Lord Jesus, and by the Spirit of our God." {I Cor.6:11} "He that is washed needeth not save to wash his feet, but is clean every whit." {Jn.13:10} "The blood of Jesus Christ his Son cleanseth us from all sin." {I Jn.1:7} "In whom we have redemption through his blood, the forgiveness of sins, according to the riches of his grace." {Eph.1:7} As sin by reason of the justice of the law of God did separate between God and us, and did make us hateful and accursed; so Christ did come to purge us from sin, {and not from the guilt and punishment alone,} which did not make God to hate us, but were rather the effects of His justice in us, and upon us. For sin, as the third Commandment sheweth, that we might be such as could justly be charged with no fault, and yet sin remaineth in the flesh, wherein is imperfection and wretchedness, and not perfection and blessedness. Why should this be strange, since God's testimony is so evident and full for it, that by reason of Christ's satisfaction all our sins are quite erased out of God's score, out of the book of His remembrance and justice, and yet that these sins are deeply and indelibly during this natural life, imprinted and fastened in our natures. As you misconceive and pervert our tenents, so your prosecution against us is lost labor.

Dr. Taylor - Page 134: "Thirdly, as he that exalts himself must be brought low; so the Scriptures show those to be in the highest estimation with God that are low, and are least in their own eyes."

R. Towne: True; but not by their own lowliness and humility, for that would have made them proud, that they were not proud. Their account and esteem with God was through Christ and His righteousness alone. Let any speak whose spirit argues or begets pride, yours or ours, whilst you make man and his works of themselves to be something to deserve regard or reward. And we according to truth teach that man is nothing, II Cor.12:11; and that all his works before or after justification; of nature, of free will, or of the Law, or faith, are as a menstrous cloth, dung, and be no cause or ground of rejoicing before God, if you consider them apart from Justification, which alone doth give them both beauty and acceptance, as is proved before. Isa.64.6, Phil.3:8, Rom.4:2. We spoil man of all matter of glorying, that he only may rejoice, and have confidence in Christ alone; and you will prune and deck him with his own ill-favored feathers, his patched, imperfect, and scanty raiment, and bid him presume to find favor and a blessing thereby at God's hands.

≡≡≡≡≡≡≡≡≡≡≡≡≡≡≡≡≡≡≡≡≡

Dr. Taylor - Page 135: "But we never read those vain voices from any truly regenerate, I am perfect, &c."

R. Towne: Yet, as Luther, so the Scriptures are full of such phrases, as some of them are, and yet they arise not from pride. If faith claim and challenge what is freely given and imparted to it by God in his word, are you so spiced with Popery, as to impute this to her sauciness and presumption? You believe a holy catholic Church, pure, perfect and undefiled, but not that you personally are so. You believe that Christ is yours, but not his perfection and blessedness, &c.? How is this pride? Your flimsy words which you throw about on purpose to make both the truth and us vile and hateful to the world, are wickedly annexed to what the Scripture doth speak and allow.

≡≡≡≡≡≡≡≡≡≡≡≡≡≡≡≡≡≡≡≡

Dr. Taylor - Page 135: "True grace {you surely would say humility, which Augustine calleth the 1,2 & 3 of grace} would keep the heart from these high strains of pride."

R. Towne: I wish yourself were not too much puffed up in your fleshly mind; for I am sure that while I view your doctrine and practice, the one tending to nothing else but to breed and nourish arrogance and contempt, though in a pretense and show of humility, and the other amounts to no less. Indeed, Augustine is of that mind, that the chief thing required or commanded in Christian religion is humility, and so thitherto if they be rightly understood, tend our tenents, but not that a man should be partially humbled, confessing that in many things he is faulty, and deserveth to be punished; but if he might be spared, he hopeth and promiseth to amend. No; this is no true knowledge of a man's self; but then is man rightly subdued indeed, when he is not only a sinner, but even sin itself, a child of wrath, and so broken in pieces, that he sees neither goodness, nor strength at all in himself, and therefore is forced to lie in his blood, confusion, and condemnation, until free grace by Jesus Christ does rescue and save him. So that all action for life and happiness faileth; for thus saith Augustine again, "let no man flatter himself, of his own he is a devil, and what maketh him happy is only from God, for what hast thou of thine own but sin, &c."

Again, in Psalm 70, he forbids us to remember our own righteousness, to the intent we may acknowledge the righteousness of God, &c., he sheweth that God so commendeth his own grace unto us, that we may know ourselves to be nothing; hence, our humiliation is Christ's exaltation. Now whether your active or your passive blessedness argues more humility, let any judge who hath skill.

Besides, your accusation and aspersion is as false as odious, for you reason not to the point in question, but pervert the state of it. See how in the like paradoxes propounded by Luther, where he affirms two seeming contraries, to wit, first, that a Christian man is a most free lord of all, and subject to none; and secondly, that a Christian man is a most dutiful servant of all, and truly subject to all. He that is not wise and wary to distinguish far better between faith and love, and what is due and peculiar to one, not to ascribe to the other, but shall inconsiderately, or in a lawless liberty of discourse, argue and conclude from the one against the other, and so he will presently overthrow and deny both. So here a Christian, when his eyes are seriously and alone upon himself, findeth no good, but a world of vanity and wickedness, a corrupt and unceasingly sinning nature, a hell of darkness, horror and despair; whence cometh such like complaints; "O wretched man that I am, who shall deliver me from the body of this death," {like to Israel being stung and inflamed with the fiery serpents,} how base and abject is he now in his spirit, anon his eyes and thoughts be raised and quickened to a lively and joyful apprehension of his perfect cleansing, plenteous redemption, plenary and everlasting victory, and salvation in Jesus Christ, {as Israel was healed and cured by looking to the brazen serpent.} What is his voice and the language now? He believeth, and therefore he speaketh; now he knoweth, and saith, but I am washed, I am justified, &c., I Cor.6:11; I am accepted in the Beloved. Eph.1:6. Truly our fellowship is with the Father, and with his Son Jesus Christ. I Jn.1:3. Thanks be to God through our Lord Jesus Christ. Rom.7:25. If you had well pondered that imperfection, yea nothing else in ourselves considered apart from Christ, and absolute perfection and fullness in Christ, do fitly accord together, yea and when that speech is of a Christian, he is properly to be conceived of, as he is in relation to Christ, hath communion and communicateth with him in all Spiritual Blessings, Eph.1:3, and that only faith by the alone help and light of the Gospel, can discern and attain this, you then surely would not have been so sharp and rash in your censor?

## Chapter VII

*Dr. Taylor's Seventh Chapter.*

≡≡≡≡≡≡≡≡≡≡≡≡≡≡≡≡≡≡≡≡

Dr. Taylor - Page 137: "Discovering the third ground, &c., affection of liberty."

R. Towne: It is liberty indeed which we attest, and unto which as its proper mark and end our doctrine tendeth, but it's only the liberty of Christ. "Stand fast therefore in the liberty wherewith Christ hath made us free, and be not entangled again with the yoke of bondage." {Gal.5:1} And whosoever receiveth it truly, learneth it effectually, and so stands fast therein, he doth find experimentally, that he is free indeed, Jn.8:36; in conscience he is discharged of his debt and burden, rid of his fears, and delivered from the power and condemnation of the Law, from the wrath of God, and out of the hands of all his enemies; in his condition, he is secure and at rest; in his calling free from distrustful, distracting and heart eating thoughts and cares; in his affections, he is sweetly seasoned and inclined to love God and man, and to testify the same in the joyful running in the ways of the Lord. These be the fruits of this righteousness of faith, as every believing soul will bear witness, as Joshua and Caleb did of the promised land, however the infidelity and malice of a great multitude, have brought bad and false reports upon the same.

≡≡≡≡≡≡≡≡≡≡≡≡≡≡≡≡≡≡≡≡≡

Dr. Taylor - Page 137: "Pride rests not in those low and humble principles."

R. Towne: Not where blessedness is passive, and man have no hand or stroke in procuring the same; but it cannot but possess and indwell the heart to imagine that life and happiness be given upon condition of man's holy and good life. Mark well what the doctrine of our Church saith, "the Doctrine of life and salvation freely without works advances the true glory of Christ, and beateth down the vainglory of man; this whosoever denieth is not to be counted for a Christian man, nor a setter forth of Christ's glory, but for an adversary to Christ and his Gospel, and for a setter forth of man's glory."

≡≡≡≡≡≡≡≡≡≡≡≡≡≡≡≡≡≡≡≡≡

Dr. Taylor - Page 139: "Rejects all rules of holy and strict walking with God."

R. Towne: Enoch, Noah, Abraham &c., walked with God as friends, by virtue of faith only in this Righteousness of Christ, and not in their own holiness of works, and performances. Can you have communion with God, except by Christ and in Christ; and is there any other way or means of embracing Christ than by faith? Let the world judge, what is the danger and consequence of your doctrine, who call upon men to walk with God in their holiness of works, which vanisheth away at the presence of God, like the morning dew. Hosea 6:4.

≡≡≡≡≡≡≡≡≡≡≡≡≡≡≡≡≡≡≡≡

Dr. Taylor - Page 139: "What will it avail to establish a faith that is dead?"

R. Towne: If you have any acquaintance either with us or our doctrine, how is it that you cease not to condemn the innocent? But whilst the Law and not the Gospel is powerful and operative with you and your hearers, to incline and move you to do what you do, who sees not what a dead and vain faith is preached and professed by you? Set blindness and malice aside, and then both sides, yours and ours, which are for works and holiness of life, in the due place, the only difference here is whether the doctrine of the Gospel or the Law makes fruitful therein. "But we all, with open face beholding as in a glass the glory of the Lord, are changed into the same image from glory to glory, even as by the Spirit of the Lord." {II Cor.3:18}

≡≡≡≡≡≡≡≡≡≡≡≡≡≡≡≡≡≡≡≡

Dr. Taylor - Page 139: "It will not be amiss to look into their model of new divinity."

R. Towne: Nay, it is most ancient, like the good wheat sown by God himself, before your tares came to be mingled with it. "Thus saith the LORD, stand ye in the ways, and see, and ask for the old paths, where is the good way, and walk therein, and ye shall find rest for your souls." {Jer.6:16}

≡≡≡≡≡≡≡≡≡≡≡≡≡≡≡≡≡≡≡≡≡≡

Dr. Taylor - Page 140: "They must not live in the presence of God."

R. Towne: Yes, being justified, we are admitted into the favor and presence of God, Rom.5:1, I Jn.1:3, there to live and abide forever through Christ our Mediatorial Representative and Advocate with the Father, by faith laying hold upon eternal life, I Tim.6:12; and therefore we conceive of him accordingly, as he hath manifested himself, to wit, not our sins, but the Righteousness of his Son is had in everlasting sight and remembrance with him. "But this shall be the covenant that I will make with the house of Israel; after those days, saith the LORD, I will put my law in their inward parts, and write it in their hearts; and will be their God, and they shall be my people. And they shall teach no more every man his neighbour, and every man his brother, saying, Know the LORD; for they shall all know me, from the least of them unto the greatest of them, saith the LORD; for I will forgive their iniquity, and I will remember their sin no more." {Jer.31:33-34} And that he hath through the blood of his Son, done away the evil of all our actions from before him, that so he may preserve them in everlasting favor. Your query favors of great ignorance of the nature and power of free Justification, and plainly betrays and argues a strong spirit of bondage.

≡≡≡≡≡≡≡≡≡≡≡≡≡≡≡≡≡≡≡≡

Dr. Taylor - Page 140: "They must not acknowledge that God rewards his own Grace."

R. Towne: It is absolutely sufficient that God gives us the reward of the merits and righteousness of Christ; and what his Spirit works in us, is wrought freely. What we by the virtue thereof are enabled to do is imperfect and defiled through the corruption of the flesh, and therefore deserves a curse rather than a blessing; but are you so mercenary, that like a crafty merchant with God, you do all for your own gain, thinking to retain favor and procure reward by good deeds; yet if you be so servile, can you in hope of reward become gods, and do good at your own pleasure? Know that such fruit is better to man's sight than to God's taste and acceptance.

≡≡≡≡≡≡≡≡≡≡≡≡≡≡≡≡≡≡≡≡

Dr. Taylor - Page 140: "They must not see their sin as a violation of the Law."

R. Towne: They are not unwilling to see the greatness and danger of their wounds, or the deepness and mystery of the Law, for both they desire to become more vile in their own eyes, and continually to die to themselves, as to all other things and works, that alone they may live in the Righteousness of Christ to God for ever. "For I through the law am dead to the law, that I might live unto God. I am crucified with Christ; nevertheless I live; yet not I, but Christ liveth in me; and the life which I now live in the flesh I live by the faith of the Son of God, who loved me, and gave himself for me." {Gal.2:19-20}

Dr. Taylor - Page 140: "God's will moves them not, because they are free from all Law."

R. Towne: Do you know nothing of God's will, but what is revealed in the Law, then his mind is that all shall perish forever. "The LORD will not spare him, but then the anger of the LORD and his jealousy shall smoke against that man, and all the curses that are written in this book shall lie upon him, and the LORD shall blot out his name from under heaven." {Deut.29:20} "For as many as are of the works of the law are under the curse; for it is written, Cursed is every one that continueth not in all things which are written in the book of the law to do them." {Gal.3:10} The will and affections of a believer according to the measure of faith, and the Spirit received, sweetly quickens, and bends to choose, affect and delight in whatever is good and acceptable to God. "For ye were sometimes darkness, but now are ye light in the Lord; walk as children of light; for the fruit of the Spirit is in all goodness and righteousness and truth; proving what is acceptable unto the Lord." {Eph.5:8-10} "But the fruit of the Spirit is love, joy, peace, longsuffering, gentleness, goodness, faith, meekness, temperance; against such there is no law. And they that are Christ's have crucified the flesh with the affections and lusts. If we live in the Spirit, let us also walk in the Spirit." {Gal.5:22-25}

≡ ≡ ≡ ≡ ≡ ≡ ≡ ≡ ≡ ≡ ≡ ≡ ≡ ≡ ≡ ≡ ≡ ≡ ≡ ≡ ≡

Dr. Taylor - Page 141: "They cannot be sick of evil motions, nor detest evil thoughts, &c."

R. Towne: Who can so hate and strive against sin, even at the first rising or stirring of it, as the believer in Christ? Can he have a continual care that Christ may dwell in him, and he abide in

Christ, Eph.3:17, and yet have an unclean heart? All evil groweth out of the bitter root of unbelief, and all good ariseth from true faith. Who then can possibly be careful in seeking the decay and weakening of the one, and the strengthening and nourishing of the other, and yet be rightly counted irreligious? "They are not accountable, say you, for any sin." O, what a blind Papistical spirit envelops your mind! Is a man justified, and yet accountable for sin, or doth not God see all erased out of his book? As Christ was tempted from without, so is the believer both from within and without, even from the evil of concupiscence; but the Spirit of Christ must needs cause both a hatred and resistance thereof. Rom.7:19. O, thou evil and slanderous tongue, these all be sufficiently proved to be calumniations and reproaches. Only that is too gross to be so slightly passed over, where you say that we revile such as call men to sanctification, &c. Your ground, manner and end, may well be excepted against; and indeed you do thereby by direct consequence destroy the article of true Justification; for your argument is too weak to procure us to be haters or resisters of true holiness of life; because we oppose and speak against your legal counterfeit and bastard like sanctification.

≡ ≡ ≡ ≡ ≡ ≡ ≡ ≡ ≡ ≡ ≡ ≡ ≡ ≡ ≡ ≡ ≡ ≡ ≡ ≡ ≡

Dr. Taylor - Page 141: "God's Spirit is all in all, and we have nothing to do. Answer: The Spirit works not without the use of means, &c."

R. Towne: This objection I am persuaded is of your own making and molding, and how maketh your answer against us, I know not; therefore shoot again.

≡ ≡ ≡ ≡ ≡ ≡ ≡ ≡ ≡ ≡ ≡ ≡ ≡ ≡ ≡ ≡ ≡ ≡ ≡ ≡ ≡

Dr. Taylor - Page 150: "Christ is our Righteousness, therefore what use have we of any of our own? Answer: Christ is not the Righteousness of Justification to any person that is not washed. I Cor.6:11."

R. Towne: I desire to construe your words in the best sense, so you mean that Christ sanctifies all whom he justifies; but yet you grant, surely, that as Justification is in order of nature the former, so it finds man in his pollution unwashed, but leaves him not so. Rom.4:5. For if we live in the Spirit, let us also walk in the Spirit. No disagreement here.

≡≡≡≡≡≡≡≡≡≡≡≡≡≡≡≡≡≡≡≡

Dr. Taylor - Page 151: "What can be added to perfection, for we are complete in Christ? Answer: Perfection is a dream."

R. Towne: The Apostle was not in a dream, Col.2:10, where {if you believe Calvin} Paul tells us, that the whole Godhead resideth in Christ; that having obtained him, we may possess also solid perfection in him; therefore saith he, those are two ways injurious to God, who do not rest in Christ alone, for beside that, they derogate from God's glory in desiring something beyond his perfection; they are ungrateful also in seeking for that elsewhere, which they have already in Christ. Yet; though we hold a perfection in Christ, we are yet against perfection in the flesh; we hold according to the Scriptures and orthodox divines a perfection of the state and condition, and yet an imperfection of faith and apprehension. What you say, only argues a defect in knowledge and apprehension, and consequently infers a diligence in the use of the means, that we may apprehend more perfectly which is never denied.

≡≡≡≡≡≡ ≡≡≡≡≡≡≡≡≡≡≡≡≡

Dr. Taylor - Page 151: "But we are called to the liberty of the Gospel, &c. Answer: What kind of liberty this is, we have seen already."

R. Towne: We teach that the Spirit of Christ leads freely and cheerfully in all the ways of God. Your lawless spirit is still wide, and beside the rule of the Law, in condemning us of Antinomianism, which we detest and oppose with as much zeal as yourself; and you err in saying, that a sweet peace and ease in the soul is grounded upon a free and sincere regard and love of the commandments, for true peace is the immediate and proper effect of Justification. "Therefore being justified, by faith we have peace with God through our Lord Jesus Christ." {Rom.5:1} "Now the God of hope fill you with all joy and peace in believing, that ye may abound in hope, through the power of the Holy Ghost." {Rom.15:13} "Come unto me, all ye that labour and are heavy laden, and I will give you rest." {Mt.11:28} But I fear this will prove the dead fly that mars everything; namely, that your conscionable applying of yourself to keep carefully the love of God is the mother and ground of your peace and security, and upon the same you wax bold to lay claim to Christ and Salvation. Who hangs now on their own righteousness?

# Chapter VIII

*Dr. Taylor's Eight Chapter.*

≡≡≡≡≡≡≡≡≡≡≡≡≡≡≡≡≡≡≡≡≡

Dr. Taylor - Page 154: "Ye are not under the Law, but under Grace. Answer: Not under the curse but under the rule."

R. Towne: This we have had before, Luther thus explains this place, "that whosoever does good works, because the Law hath so ordained, being moved thereunto, either by fear of punishment or hope of reward, those are under the Law, and it causes them to do good and live honestly; and their own free will doth not move and incline them so to do; therefore the Law hath dominion over them, and such men are the servants and captives thereof. So that his opinion is plain, that whosoever is otherwise minded and disposed, because the Law requires it, he refrains from evil and doth good, that man is under the Law, and not under Grace. In what condition then, I pray you, are you with your followers, for your distinction is vain and groundless, as has already been showed.

≡≡≡≡≡≡≡≡≡≡≡≡≡≡≡≡≡≡≡≡≡

Dr. Taylor - Page 154: "For as many as are of the works of the law are under the curse; for it is written, Cursed is every one that continueth not in all things which are written in the book of the law to do them." {Gal.3:10} "The Apostle saith not that these to whom the Law appertains."

R. Towne: Yes, the word must necessarily impart so much, for therefore are all under the works of it, because the Law appertains to all; and therefore apart from Christ's fulfillment of the Law for some, all perish!

=========================

Dr. Taylor - Page 154: "The works of the Law are twofold, either of obedience done in humility, &c."

R. Towne: It is nothing but pride of spirit, whatever show it make of humility, when men think they can do anything rightly upon the commandment of the Law, by way of duty or thankfulness, or as a condition of life. "Without me, ye can do nothing," saith Christ.

=========================

Dr. Taylor - Page 154: "Knowing this, that the law is not made for a righteous man, but for the lawless and disobedient, for the ungodly and for sinners, &c." {I Tim.1:9} "The scope is not to abolish the Law, &c."

R. Towne: Who abolishes or seeks to impair or lessen the authority of the Law, so as do you and your followers, who pretend a Law without any power to curse, &c. Love, you say, is a fruit and effect of faith, then not of the Law, for the spirit of faith entering doth loose the heart that was taken prisoner, and lay in bondage before, sweetly enlivening and inclining it to love God and man; and so by faith bringing love, a man is freely enlarged and prepared to the duties of the Law, and is not tied and bound thereunto as a bear to the stake. Is there any comparison between the righteousness of Adam in innocence and of a believer in Christ? Adam's innocence being inherent, and finite {like himself,} and the Righteousness of Christ imputed and infinite, for it is the Righteousness of God. "For he hath made him to be sin for us, who knew no sin; that we might be made the righteousness of God in him." {II Cor.5:21} "In his days Judah shall be saved, and Israel shall dwell safely; and this is his name whereby he shall be called, THE LORD OUR RIGHTEOUSNESS." {Jer.23:6} "Surely, shall one say, in the LORD have I righteousness and strength; even to him shall men come; and all that are incensed against him shall be ashamed. In the LORD shall all the seed of Israel be justified, and shall glory." {Isa.45:24-25} Or is there any difference between their states; Adam being under a Law, as a condition of life and death, Gen.2:17, and the believer being redeemed from it. "But when the fulness of the time was come, God sent forth his Son, made of a woman, made under the law, to redeem them that were under the law, that we might receive the adoption of sons." {Gal.4:4-5} Yet, thus it is true, as Adam was under the government of the inward righteousness of his heart by virtue of his creation; so is a believer a servant of righteousness; that is, of that law of righteousness written in the heart by the faith of Justification. "Being then made free from sin, ye became the servants of righteousness." {Rom.6:18} "No weapon that is formed against thee shall prosper; and every tongue that shall rise against thee in judgment thou shalt condemn. This is the heritage of the servants of the LORD, and their righteousness is of me, saith the LORD." {Is.54:17} "But now being made free from sin, and become servants to God, ye have your fruit unto holiness, and the end everlasting life." {Rom.6:22} The antithesis used by the apostle, "for sin shall not have dominion over you; for ye are not under the law, but under grace," Rom.6:14, is remarkable. He opposeth the kingdom of Grace against the dominion of Sin and the Law, and sheweth that in our natural estate sin is so strong and forcible in us, that God hath put us under an outward law of precepts to be taught and tutored by it, &c., for we were like unto a horse and mule that must be curbed, and guided by the rider; but after Faith {Christ} is come, it subdueth and weakeneth that tyranny, it bringeth an inward spirit of righteousness which possesseth and persuadeth the heart aright, and so leadeth and ordereth the whole man in all the ways of godliness and truth. I conceive that your failing is thus, in that you endeavor after an outward reformation of manners, and yet the inward man is crooked and warped. You would have an outward authority to bow and incline the soul unto that to which it hath no affection, nor free inclination. You are ever imperiously by the commandment of the law exacting and requiring this and that with strong threatenings; it must be done, or smart for neglect &c., little considering that believers are of an ingenuous and free disposition. It cannot be said, that my spirit doth that voluntarily, which the command of the Law bindeth and forceth unto; for it is one thing for a man at his own free liberty to keep the Kings Highway of the Law; and another to be kept in by pales and ditches, that he cannot without some danger go out of it. Whilst the child is under the awe, and rule of his Tutor or Master, you cannot know his disposition, although he live soberly and orderly; but free him from that government, and leave him to himself, and you may soon know what to judge of him. This is no plea for carnal looseness, but a necessary trial to put all professors unto, that it may be seen, whether the Son hath made them free indeed or not, Jn. 3:36, for the Law doth not loose its dominion until God's Grace do predispose us to itself, that it may reveal righteousness; "therefore it's impossible that we should be thralls to sin, since the grace of God reigneth in us," saith Calvin.

  I well like Augustine's gradation, when he says that, "by the Law is the knowledge of sin, by faith is grace perceived; by grace cometh nature to be healed of the disease of sin, and hence is freedom of will, thence the love of righteousness, after that the performing of the Law, and so the Law is not made void." Paul, Zacchaeus the Publican, and all the nations of the Gentiles began to bring forth fruit when they began to be engrafted into Christ. If the spirit of a believer be free, why will you control and rule it by the Law, whereas the nature of the Spirit is freely bestowed to conform the heart and life to the outward rule of the Law without the help of the Law. As a crooked thing is made straight according to the line and square, and not by them; and thus whilst a believer serves in newness of spirit, the Spirit freely and cheerfully moving and inclining him in Gospel ways, in which he is merely passive herein; so both those do wickedly who hence take liberty to sin, and they also speak lewdly, who teach that by this means the bridle is given to our vile lusts. "For we are his workmanship, created in Christ Jesus unto good works, which God hath before ordained that we should walk in them." {Eph.2:10}

===============================

Dr. Taylor - Page 154: "It is never said that Christ hath freed us from the obedience of the Law."

R. Towne: But it must be said and granted, for Christ neither did nor could in justice free from the curse, unless first he freed from the obedience, to wit, for life and salvation. What Christ as our Surety did undertake for us, that he hath freed us from; but he undertook the obedience, even the active and passive fulfilling of all righteousness, as well as the curse. "Suffer it to be so now; for thus it becometh us to fulfil all righteousness." {Mt.3:15} "The LORD is well pleased for his righteousness' sake; he will magnify the law, and make it honourable." {Is.42:21} "Think not that I am come to destroy the law, or the prophets; I am not come to destroy, but to fulfil." {Mt.5:17}

=============================

Dr. Taylor - Page 165: "Christian liberty is not a freedom from obedience, but straightly orders it."

R. Towne: It is a freedom from all by faith, and to all in love, the effect of faith, and as faith is free, so is love, and so be her offices and duties, as is Sarah the mother, so is her son Isaac, &c., therefore away with your straight injunction. The Apostle intends a liberty from the whole government of Moses; the Lord according to his ancient purpose and promise now minding to give a more free condition and estate to his Church in the days of the Gospel, and to preserve and keep them in all righteousness under the kingdom of Grace, without the Law ceremonial or moral; your dividing of Moses's yoke, and rending of the Law into so many pieces and branches, is without warrant, but not without danger.

=============================

Dr. Taylor - Page 168: Lk.16:16 & Rom.10:4. "The Law for writing and some circumstances was given by Moses."

R. Towne: For writing, and doth not the writing of the Law appertain to us? "For whatsoever things were written aforetime were written for our learning, that we through patience and comfort of the scriptures might have hope." {Rom.15:4} These so oft sod coleworts, I say, it suffices, that whereas their Gospel and ours for substance was the same, yet believers be now freed from the pedagogue and manner of education under Moses.

You say, that Christ was the end of the moral Law, because he obeyed the Law, &c., and what Christ performed for us we are freed from; now you are with us, that is, Christ hath freed us from subjection to the Law; in whom, you say, all blessings and promises attain their end. How stands this with your reward and promises upon condition of good works; for if something be promised for your obedience, then not all to Christ, and for Christ, and consequently he is not the perfect end of the Law in this respect by your doctrine?

I see not how your conclusion here issues from these premises, but as here you unwittingly affirm the truth, so I am sure if we be faster tied to the obedience of the Law than before, we have no help by Christ, but rather he hath made our case more miserable; and this is your Gospel. Why then do you unloose the cords, and abate so much of the rigor of the Law, as your tenents cross and overthrow themselves.

≡≡≡≡≡≡≡≡≡≡≡≡≡≡≡≡≡≡≡≡≡≡≡

Dr. Taylor - Page 168: "Very false therefore is that position that the Law is at such an end, as it can no more command, &c."

R. Towne: So you say, but prove nothing. Your exposition of Romans 7:4 is far too short; the Apostle speaks expressly of the Law. The curse, and rebellious motions, &c., are not the Law. As a woman, you say, from threats, &c., this husband that neither used nor knew any mercy or favor is the Law whom the apostle means not to make gentle and merciful, and so to conjoin him again to the conscience as you intend. "But, you object, the Apostle saith not that the Law is dead in respect of direction." Neither saith he that it is alive, and of force to direct; but his words imply no less. And will you in a needless fear raise up the former dead husband to instruct and teach his wife still; being married again to one infinitely more wise and able than himself, thus you regard not how you dishonor and derogate from Christ, so that the Law have more than is due. But in your margin you show your reader, that we are dead to the Law, and the Law not dead to us, doth it not come all to one? The allegory runs most aptly thus, the Law is dead to us, and so it is like Paul would have said, to show how we are by faith freed from the authority of it, but that he was loath to offend the weak Jews, who were too zealous of the Law; yet he saith as much in verse 6, "but now we are delivered from the law, that being dead wherein we were held; that we should serve in newness of spirit, and not in the oldness of the letter;" so Calvin on Gal.2:19, saith, "that no man liveth to the Law, safe to whom the Law is dead, that is, idle and without effect."

You say, "we show the end of our freedom, &c.," but, if you rightly considered, what you write, here might be an end likewise of your fear and mistake, for who, if he ponder it well, can fear or conclude a fleshly licentiousness, where the believing soul is united and married to Christ in a spiritual bond of everlasting love and grace. The Scriptures everywhere testify, that all virtue and power to lead a godly life is communicated by Christ alone. The Law and Christ are set in opposition, as two husbands to one wife successively; whilst the Law was alive in the conscience, all the fruits were deadly and accursed, Rom.7:5, but Christ taking the same spouse to himself {the term of the Law being expired} by his quickening Spirit doth make her fruitful to God, and so raises up seed to the former husband; for materially these are the works of the Law, though produced by the Spirit of Christ in the Gospel. "Wherefore, my brethren, ye also are become dead to the law by the body of Christ; that ye should be married to another, even to him who is raised from the dead, that we should bring forth fruit unto God." {Rom.7:4} "For the hope which is laid up for you in heaven, whereof ye heard before in the word of the truth of the gospel; which is come unto you, as it is in all the world; and bringeth forth fruit, as it doth also in you, since the day ye heard of it, and knew the grace of God in truth." {Col.1:5-6}

"His shift, say you, is too short to shuffle from the first Covenant to the second." I know not whose shift it is, nor well what you intend, therefore I leave it to whom it concerns. Some be so subtle in their shifts, that they hide themselves and play least in sight, but it is not so with you, whose malady is all too manifest. Men live in the Covenant of New Testament Grace without any condition of doing, they live and then do, their life is by a life of faith, Rom.1:17; and if you had but the least spark of that love and tender regard of the Gospel, that you seem to have of the Law, you would not have left your words so obscure and doubtful.

# Chapter IX

*Dr. Taylor's Ninth Chapter.*

===========================

Suppose a justified man commits adultery, &c. The ground of the objection seemeth to be this; that in whatsoever the Law hath power to command, the same also necessarily hath power to justify and condemn as its obeyed or disobeyed, &c. But why suppose you such gross and open sins? Is it not because your mind is too pharisaical? May not the Law take hold, and the just God punish for the least blind, rash or idle thought, as well as for these? I easily espy your lower leaven. For you say; the Law both for matter and form stands in force; and to justify and condemn are as proper and essential to the Law, as to command, as has been showed already; and so the justified shall be then still under both the command and condemnation of the Law, although the manner of command in the rigor is to them abated. I would see Scripture for this, for I read and hear it often from man, but Christ saith, "that one jot or tittle shall not perish from the Law," yet if I believe you, can you certify me how far then, or how much of the rigor is abated; or can you warrantably tell me, that this is the nature and extent of the dispensation of the Law by means of the Gospel; and if I walk humbly and carefully, shall not the Law condemn me for imperfection and defect? What a dallying and mockery is this! Come to experience and practice, you are justified in Christ, and live under the directory and commanding power of the Law, but are freed {as you affirm} from the condemning power and curse, whilst you make indentures, being off and on, in and out, weak and halting in the whole course of your life, if the matter be so mitigated by God, that His Law requireth no more than you carefully can perform, &c. Wherein now do you offend? The Law is become as weak and childish as yourself, it can bear with, and wink at your slips and failings. Why do you repent? Why are you dejected at any time? Why ask you forgiveness? Why do you accuse and condemn yourselves, for God doth not, neither does his Law, &c.? You tell us of an ample and abundant favor and dispensation. What use make you of it? How idle, dangerous, and groundless is this teaching; and to what other purpose Satan hath foisted this into the Church, I know not, except to put hereby pillows under men's arms, that they may rest and sleep securely in their own good desires, and zealous endeavors to serve God, and to make no further use of justification, being quite fallen from grace. This is your doctrine, that Christ hath justified us from all the evils of our lives before our calling and conversion to the faith, having fully satisfied the Law for them, but afterwards God hath laid aside his strict and perfect Justice, and will be content with what we can and strive to do. What you infer from our tenents, as that we are against humiliation, repentance, &c., may easily and more strongly be concluded against you by this kind of teaching. "Confused men," you call us, but the strength of this vain distinction is long since departed, and therefore cannot harm us or hurt our cause.

You perform obedience, you say, not to merit. I see but a small difference between merit, as it is commonly taken, and the reward that you stand for; for the merit-mongers grant that such is the infinite distance and disproportion between the wages and our works, that in strictness of justice no such thing is deserved, yet by agreement, since the Lord hath vouchsafed to promise so largely upon condition of a small pittance of service, we may expect what is due, because of his bounty and fidelity, who hath by promise made himself a debtor. Indeed our true Protestant divines affirm that there is a reward, which is to be eyed and regarded as an encouragement to the faithful in all the exercises of piety, in tribulations and sufferings; but it is promised not to the work, but to the worker, and it is his for Christ's sake, before he performs anything; so that though he be often called upon to look upon it, that he faint not, &c., that is, to let him see that he can be no loser, though he give and lose all for Christ's sake, seeing that Christ hath obtained and purchased far greater good than these perishable vanities, and therefore we are said but to receive the end of our faith, the penny, &c., which is also called a reward, because it is given to be enjoyed at the end of our work and faith, as are the wages at the end of the day. "Wherefore seeing we also are compassed about with so great a cloud of witnesses, let us lay aside every weight, and the sin which doth so easily beset us, and let us run with patience the race that is set before us, looking unto Jesus the author and finisher of our faith." {Heb.12:1-2} "Blessed be the God and Father of our Lord Jesus Christ, which according to his abundant mercy hath begotten us again unto a lively hope by the resurrection of Jesus Christ from the dead, to an inheritance incorruptible, and undefiled, and that fadeth not away, reserved in heaven for you, who are kept by the power of God through faith unto salvation ready to be revealed in the last time. Wherein ye greatly rejoice, though now for a season, if need be, ye are in heaviness through manifold temptations; that the trial of your faith, being much more precious than of gold that perisheth, though it be tried with fire, might be found unto praise and honour and glory at the appearing of Jesus Christ; whom having not seen, ye love; in whom, though now ye see him not, yet believing, ye rejoice with joy unspeakable and full of glory; receiving the end of your faith, even the salvation of your souls." {I Pet.1:3-9}

≡≡≡≡≡≡≡≡≡≡≡≡≡≡≡≡≡≡≡≡

Dr. Taylor - Page 178: "Say you, that God's Law taketh no hold of a justified person, and this is utterly false."

R. Towne: Yes I say, and find daily, that God's law taketh hold on the conscience, to convince, rebuke and terrify, not only for gross offenses, but for the least failing; yea, for the imperfection of the best thing that ever he doth, till Christ our continual Refuge doth deliver the conscience. "How much more shall the blood of Christ, who through the eternal Spirit offered himself without spot to God, purge your conscience from dead works to serve the living God?" {Heb.9:14} Let the Law then be still in full force and authority, and its usefulness to a Christian, for I know none that teach otherwise; thus it driveth to Christ, keepeth the soul close, that it dare not look away from his Righteousness, or depart from faith, to mind and regard his best performances, for fear of condemnation.

≡≡≡≡≡≡≡≡≡≡≡≡≡≡≡≡≡≡≡≡≡

Dr. Taylor - Page 178: "But of all their assertions, that is, as blind and bold, God hath nothing to do to call him to account."

R. Towne: If such speeches have fallen from any, your character might make a good construction of them, for you know that there is a holy boldness, and a plea of faith, a drawing near "with a true heart in full assurance of faith, having our hearts sprinkled from an evil conscience," Heb.10:22, which conscience makes answer to God; that is, "the answer of a good conscience toward God, by the resurrection of Jesus Christ," I Pet.3:21, saying in the like case, "thy Son, O, God hath died for me, he had undergone the weight of thy wrath, &c., what more canst thou require of me, &c." Also, what is more useful in the prayers of preachers than such words as these, "but we appeal from thy justice to the throne of mercy &c.," as refusing to be tried in that Court, and yourself do witness again and again, that the condemnation of the Law hath nothing to do with the believer, which is the same in effect, for he doth not stand and fall to God upon such terms. This is the privilege and lawful plea of faith, useful and necessary in time of temptation, urging God with his own promise, relying confidently and soberly upon the Covenant of Free Grace without works, &c., therefore desiring to remove the whole Law of works out of sight in this conflict; and it ought not, being spoken in reverence and sobriety of spirit, to be called a saucy telling of God what to do, but rather the humble claim, acknowledgment, and use of that consolation and liberty which God graciously affords to distressed minds; but so lamentable are the times, that what savors of true Christian liberty and faith, will not be relished and digested, when it is delivered in the most submissive and compassionate manner, much less after this downright and peremptory fashion.

≡≡≡≡≡≡≡≡≡≡≡≡≡≡≡≡≡≡≡≡≡

Dr. Taylor - Page 178: "The former proposition is false, that those that have the Spirit, have no need of the Law."

R. Towne: The Spirit orders, disposes and moves the heart to faith and love; the Law is useful for the expression and manifestation of them; for if I love God and my neighbor, I can testify it only by the works of the Law; but you strangely conclude a contrary, from what in truth argues a sweet harmony and unity between the Holy Spirit of God within us, and the Law, into the way whereof we are guided freely and cheerfully, for the proposition implies an agreement, and you infer a contradiction. "These are inseparable," say you, but how inseparable? The Spirit is free and blows where and when it listeth, Jn.3:8, and doth not always necessarily accompany the word; therefore the fishers of men many times catch nothing. Besides, we are to distinguish both between the doctrine of the Law and the Gospel, and the operations of the Spirit; for as the Spirit uses and works by the Law, so it is called the spirit of bondage, Rom.8:15, causing fear, for it causes sin to revive, and presents to the conscience its misery and thralldom; and the Apostle saith, that the Law worketh wrath, Rom.4:15, and is the ministry of condemnation, II Cor.3:9; but the same Spirit reveals and communicates righteousness, adoption, liberty, consolation, life, and sanctification, by the instrument or ministry of the Gospel. "Who also hath made us able ministers of the New Testament; not of the letter, but of the spirit; for the letter killeth, but the spirit giveth life. But if the ministration of death, written and engraven in stones, was glorious, so that the children of Israel could not steadfastly behold the face of Moses for the glory of his countenance; which glory was to be done away; how shall not the ministration of the Spirit be rather glorious." {II Cor.3:6-8} "For I am not ashamed of the gospel of Christ; for it is the power of God unto salvation to everyone that believeth; to the Jew first, and also to the Greek. For therein is the righteousness of God revealed from faith to faith; as it is written, the just shall live by faith." {Rom.1:16-17} "This only would I learn of you, received ye the Spirit by the works of the law, or by the hearing of faith?" {Gal.3:2} The Law divulges the darkness, hardness and insensibleness of heart, to bring to a true sight and feeling that desperate wound of sin; but the Gospel is the healing plaster, curing its patients in a way of justification and sanctification. Hence Augustine says rightly, "the disease is discovered by the Law, but is healed by the Grace of the Gospel."

You call us Antinomians and Enthusiasts, but in a blind mistake, you regard not among whom you number us, only you gladly would take any occasion to show your spleen and ill will, and to make us hateful to all, but in calumnies of spirit judge righteously, whether the denying of the Law to be an instrument of sanctification doth argue a rejecting of all means, &c. Enough hath been said to refuel your sinister conceits, to clear the truth, and us, and to satisfy any indifferent mind, and as you object to no new thing, so you have had your answer before.

===============================

Dr. Taylor - Page 184: "Those that are under the Law of Christ are not under the moral Law."

R. Towne: As I am a stranger to this objection, so I will not curiously scan the distinction in the exposition, for none will deny this surely. That by your natural and first birth we are all under the Law, for we are by nature the children of wrath, Eph.2:3; and, that as Christ hath saved us from this wrath and freed us from that fearful condition, so he hath redeemed us from the Law. "But when the fulness of the time was come, God sent forth his Son, made of a woman, made under the law, to redeem them that were under the law, that we might receive the adoption of sons." {Gal.4:4-5}

The proposition, you say, is false, &c., seeing the Law of Christ is for substance the same, &c. I see no falsity discovered by your ground. For if by substance you mean that both these laws are of one and the same essence, nature or yet office, you are far wide. Gal.3:10-13. And, if as I think you intend, that the subject matter of both is the same, and that because both contain and require righteousness, Rom.1:17, therefore it is all one to be under the one or the other. Your argument will not hold, and this shall suffice for now, for though the Law imperiously command, yet we are impotent and beggarly, and it will not relieve and help us; but the Gospel is bountiful to all the subjects thereof, it freely giveth all necessaries to salvation and happiness. The Law requires that we do and give unto God; the Gospel teaches us to believe, and to take or receive all freely from God. Is this no difference between being under the one and the other? Look no further than your text, Rom.6:14, that the Romans feared that sin would subdue and enthrall them. The Apostle grants that if they were under the Law, it would sooner strengthen than weaken the power of sin; but being under the Grace of the Gospel, he will warrant and secure them against the dominion of sin.

========================

Dr. Taylor - Page 185: "For what is the Law of Christ, but the commandment of Christ enjoining the love of our brethren, &c."

R. Towne: True, this is Christ's Law touching our conversation in the world, but not our Salvation with God. It is his Law effectively not formally, for this is his commandment, that we should believe on his name; and the effect of this faith is love. It is his Law for the expression of our love; but not to beget the inward affection thereof. Gal.5:6.

========================

Dr. Taylor - Page 186: "Which the Apostle, say you, opposes not to the moral Law."

R. Towne: The Apostle opposes the doctrine of the Gospel against the whole pedagogical government under Moses, which comprehendeth the moral as well as the ceremonial Law; and so Luther, Calvin, Beza and Perkins make it clear, to whom Zanchy also upon Galatians agrees, saying, that the general state of the question, and dispute between Paul and the false apostles, who sought to pervert the Gospel, and did tamper with the Galatians as with other churches, was this, whether besides faith in Christ, the works also of the Law were necessary to Salvation. Paul affirmed that faith or grace alone did justify and save, but they taught a union and concurrence of both grace and works to be necessary. Note by the way, how you jump with those seducers as well as the papists, when you conjoin repentance and sincere obedience, with faith in the work of redemption; and first you require faith, as did also the seducers. Acts 15:5. And then you subjoin the other two, as they did the circumcision, and the keeping of the Law of Moses; which thing, Paul called a perverting and destroying of the true Gospel, and was the ground and cause of their apostasy. Against which kind of doctrine, in imitation of that blessed Apostle, I shall ever profess myself an opposite.

≡≡≡≡≡≡ ≡≡≡≡≡≡≡≡≡≡≡≡≡

Dr. Taylor - Page 186: "It is frivolous and popish, you say, to conceive the Gospel a new Law."

R. Towne: Simply to conceive the Gospel as a new Law, that is, a divers Law or doctrine from the Decalogue is neither frivolous nor popish, for it is called a New Covenant, Heb.8:8, and a new commandment. Jn.13:34. I do not see why you should clap this on our backs, and do wonder if the Law arrest you not for a false accusation; for the objection mentions no such thing, and your own sense and practice will prove yourself guilty.

    You ask, is not the Covenant of Grace the same? Yes, in substance, but not in manner of dispensation; but is this any reason to prove that we make the Gospel a new Law, or that the papists do err in so doing; or to what end, you say, thus I discern not. Did not the Apostle to free his doctrine from suspicion of novelty, say it is the old commandment, &c., I Jn.2:7, that is none other than was taught and given in charge at the first broaching of the Gospel; and yet he adds, that it is a new commandment too, not only because it is enforced from a new ground, and revealed as you write, but in that also, it is given after a new manner; for as it is enjoined by the moral Law, it's only literal and external; but Christ by the doctrine of faith, which is the ministration of the Spirit, II Cor.3:7-9, doth effectually write it in the table of the heart; and thus he renews this commandment of love, but not after the nature of a Law, but through the Gospel by which he giveth himself to our faith, that so being believed on, he may claim us as sons of God, pardon our sins, purge out the remnants of the flesh, and so bring forth in us true love towards our brethren. "But as many as received him, to them gave he power to become the sons of God, even to them that believe on his name; which were born, not of blood, nor of the will of the flesh, nor of the will of man, but of God." {Jn.1:12-13} It is also for a new, that is, another end; the Law requires love, that we might live, find peace, favor and salvation; but the Gospel exhorts unto it, because we are justified and saved freely, and to be followers of Christ, Eph.5:1-2, to declare how truly the love of God is shed abroad in our hearts, &c. What follows is all of the same hatch, so that I may well forbear further enlargement.

# Chapter X

≡≡≡≡≡≡≡≡≡≡≡≡≡≡≡≡≡≡≡≡≡

Whosoever shall diligently pursue and weigh this treatise of our just and necessary defense will plainly perceive himself, I doubt not, from the very beginning of it hitherto, to be carried freely and clearly by the pure stream both of Divine and human testimonies; so that his own experience will be a sufficient shield for us against the indignity of this last accusation; for if the doctor himself had not been so foully guilty of wresting and perverting our words and meaning, and of sophistically inferring undue and indirect conclusions from sound and orthodox premises and tenets, he would have never numbered us amongst Antinomians, Abrogaters of the Law, Libertines, &c., neither could he have impanelled his jury of divines against us; but whilst he wickedly both mistakes and miscalls us, his error is condemned by all, and we are acquitted. His indictment and bill of information is black and foul, but what he hath proved, whereof stand we convicted either in conscience or in the open court of man. For if by any one syllable of solid argument he hath made it appear that we are the men that he hath noted us for, then are we cast and condemned; otherwise we fear neither amerce nor verdict, knowing that his bare word, nor yet his ranting, reviling and reproachful speeches will be held any proof. We will say, and are ready being called, to make it further appear, that we have the consent and authority not of some, but of all the Protestant writers that we have seen of any note, to strengthen and confirm all that we hold or teach; and what you falsely charge us withal, returns upon your own head, look to it, for "the righteousness of the righteous shall be upon him, and the wickedness of the wicked shall be upon him." {Ez.18:20} Your testimonies are against the Antinomians, the Abrogaters of the Law, &c., we also do condemn and disclaim all of that opinion and sect, thus in despite of your ill will, we still agree with your authors. Answer directly, do these or other Protestant divines which you verse in deny: 1. That whatever is done before Justification is sin. 2. That blessedness is passive. 3. That Justification, which is the absolution from all sins original, actual, past, present, and to come, and the imputation of an everlasting righteousness doth make our state and condition absolute and entire. 4. That our peace, favor, adoption, communion with God and his saints, sanctification, and glorification, are the sole effects and fruits of faith in the said Justification. 5. That perfection is the ground of acceptance, both of our persons and performances. 6. That to return to works, with an opinion that the free Grace of Christ is not sufficient to Justification and Salvation, unless you join the keeping of the Law, is to abrogate Grace, and to fall away from the faith, and to make Christ's death void. 7. That believers are one with Christ, are already saved in him, being set together with him in heavenly places, where they possess blessedness, immortality and glory. 8. That Salvation as well as Justification is free and without works. Or do they not deny: 1. That our tears wash away sin. 2. That repentance, humiliation, promise, purpose, and carefulness to amend our lives, can pacify wrath, or procure peace with God, ascribing as the truth is, this alone to the grace of Christ. 3. That man can become good by doing of good. 4. That the Law is the seed or doctrine of regeneration or the new birth. 5. That the best works after Justification in themselves considered do displease God, because of their imperfection; and that they only become graceful and acceptable in Christ. 6. That the Law is the instrument of the Spirit in working true sanctification, but the Gospel only. 7. The Law is abrogated; but contrariwise they affirm, that is, rightly established by this doctrine, and so they condemn your false, absurd and damnable inferences and calumniations.

As the door hangs and turns on its hinges, so it is well known that the quarrel and controversy between the doctor with his accomplices, and us, is, mainly upon these named grounds. London will witness that those whose credit, along with his own, that he so labors to redeem and salve have directly opposed both the doctrine of our Church, and of other learned judicious and orthodox divines in us in these points, both in the pulpit and in private conference; but the wit of the doctor serves him to pass these over, save some few which he touches in a shuffling and confused manner; and he and his associates can take no other course to prevent their own confusion, which the faithful publishing of these will inevitably bring upon their ministry, than by making us vile and contemptible by that most false, wicked and unchristian imputations. Well, whosoever is wise will ponder these things in question, and make them the touchstone and trial of the doctrine of our times; and for a closure of this chapter I say again, that when the doctor proves us Antinomians, &c., then there will be use of this jury, but until then they may stand honest, learned and revered men and fathers as they be.

# Chapter XI

≡≡≡≡≡≡≡≡≡≡≡≡≡≡≡≡≡≡≡≡≡≡

This chapter he spends in the application of his doctrine, and so it contains only a repetition of what formally is answered; yet to make up his number of chapters, having some spare time and paper both, I will somewhat enlarge myself in further clearing and confirming of two points in question, which the doctor often mentioned and glanced at, but either was unwilling or accounted it needless thoroughly to discuss and handle, and of purpose I forbear to say more, then might retell his objections, as occasion still was given, because I intended a more punctual and particular confirmation of them. I have many inducements hereunto; as first I hear those two spoken against in every place; secondly, the state of the questions are first perverted and wrested, and then condemned; thirdly, then by these thus deformed by themselves, they bid to guess at the rest; fourthly, they are points that be rarely spoken of, except in this envious and sinister manner; fifthly, in reading they are by few duly observed; sixthly, the simpler minded, through an easy mistake, stumble at them; seventhly, the main current and practice of the ministry is utterly against them; eighthly, the errors and evils which spring from the ignorance and condemning of them are manifold and intolerable; ninthly, also by reason of them, it pleases our adversaries to brand us with the names of Perfectionists, Enthusiasts, Antinomians, Familists, Libertines, &c. We only desire leave to speak for ourselves before we be censured. This method I shall observe; first, I will lay down the propositions; secondly, show upon what occasion they came to be questioned;

thirdly, the ground and warrant of our assertion; fourthly, lastly I shall answer what objections are obvious and useful against the same.

The propositions are these: 1. A believer is as well saved already, as justified by Christ, and in him. 2. That the Gospel is the ordinary instrument of sanctification, and not the Law.

The occasion of the former was this. In a private conference in London it was said, that a believer ought exceedingly to rejoice, in that he was so freely justified and saved. Against which a minister excepted, saying, that he was justified but not saved as yet, and being urged with Scripture which testified the one as well as the other; he replied, that it was true in regard of hope, and of some beginnings of Salvation, and no otherwise; and further he threatened to bring his opponent in before authority, unless he would recant what he had said. It was answered that Zanchy, had these words, that the Colossians not only might receive from Christ what pertains to Salvation and perfection, but that they had it already, and were now complete in Christ. He replied, it was false, for Zanchy wrote not upon the Colossians, and offered wagers, &c., but after refused. In fine, a meeting was concluded upon, that authors might be consulted with, and after that a moderator was chosen, yet nothing could be affected, for the said Minister published it to all, and so it was reported that we held perfection in the flesh, &c. A letter was sent to the minister in defense of the tenent, which he would never as yet answer, the copy whereof followeth word for word.

Grace and Peace, you remember the points in question between both of us, and how they were occasioned; now, however others may deem, there is nothing that I hate and seek to prevent more after my mean condition and talent, then rents and divisions in the Church. Therefore remembering at our last meeting, your ingenuous protestation, that your contending was not for victory, but for the sifting and clearing of the Truth, I am thereby the rather induced freely to offer to your judicious consideration, what grounds and reasons I have for my assertions from sacred Scripture, and approved authors. It is true, that I hold that first question affirmatively, even as it was stated by you, that is, whether a believer may be properly said to be presently saved in this life {that is} in Christ; as I always said, for I hold no perfection in the flesh, &c., and that because of these Scriptures. Jn.3:36; Jn.5:24; Col.2:10; Eph.1:3; Eph.2:5-8; Heb.10:14; Tit.3:5; I Jn.5:11-12; Phil.3:12, &c. It is a marvel how the credit of these words can stand, wherein the Apostle affirms, that we are already saved, although living yet on earth, and therefore in continual warfare and misery, &c., wherefore all the life of the Christian after faith is nothing else but an expectation of Salvation and Felicity to be revealed, which they that believe in Christ, do now possess, although hidden, they having all things now certainly in their Redeemer. We must consider our Salvation in two ways; first, in Christ our Head, in whom we have not attained one or more parts, but full Salvation; and secondly, as it is in ourselves, not as though already attained, either already perfected; but following after, if that we may apprehend that for which also we are apprehended of Christ Jesus. {Phil.3:12}

    Sir, I desire nothing more than to see my error, if I have failed, for I grant and confess also that many divines say, that life and salvation is but here inchoate, but I conceive, here is the difference, for they speak then of life as it is here in us subjectively, whereas these, along with many other authors, consider it as it is in Christ. "For in him dwelleth all the fulness of the Godhead bodily. And ye are complete in him." {Col.2:10} Also, it is true, that we are said, as you objected, to be saved by hope, Rom.8:24, and so Christ is our righteousness, by which we are now perfectly justified, as you hold, said to be the object of hope, Gal.5:5, and our adoption, Rom.8:23; yet we are now the sons of God, I Jn.3:2; and our complete redemption is by Christ, Lk.1:68, for Christ is the treasure of the Church; but you know that the way of reconciling these Scriptures, for Christ alone makes certain of these treasures, and hope waits for possession, for hope hath certainty as well as faith, and therefore it makes not ashamed, Rom.5:5, and also he that believes hath eternal life. Jn.3:36. But thus I have learned it, that faith and hope differ; first, in their offices, as faith apprehends and hope expects; secondly, in their object, for justification, reconciliation, adoption, glorification and eternal life reside in Christ; and it is true, that in respect of our sense and apprehension, there is a difference between the state of grace and glory; for here in this life, our faith and knowledge is imperfect; but in Christ who is our Covenant Representative and Eternal Surety we stand complete. If I could more plainly and briefly lay open my meaning, surely, I would, for God is my witness, that I hold nothing which I will not gladly impart and submit to better judgment. I think the other question is no less obscure, and therefore to avoid repetition, I shall omit it till another time, when you think fit. Dec.14, 1630; yours as you will call or use him, Robert Towne.

≡≡≡≡≡≡ ≡≡≡≡≡≡≡≡≡≡≡≡≡≡

Omitting the rest, what could be produced more fit and full to the point in question, then those words both of Paul, Eph.2:5, and of Beza upon the same, testifying that the Apostle saith not, ye began to be saved, or ye shall be saved, but ye are already saved. Also, those are the words of

Musculus {unto whom the letter referred him,} upon Ephesians chapter 2. In Christ we are already in heavenly places, and so sit at the right hand of the Father, and do obtain all the glory of the heavenly kingdom, &c. Again, it ought to be a thing of the greatest moment to us, that the Apostle saith, that God hath already quickened, raised and placed us at his right hand in heavenly places, even then, when he raised his Son Jesus Christ from the dead, and made him sit and reign at his right hand in heaven; for how should that not be, or how can that be made void, which God already hath wrought for us in his Son? Before him we are all, that which he willed, and also hath caused us to be, Christ is not alone in his eyes, and on his right hand, but we also are conjoined to him, &c. Who desires further satisfaction, may read the said author.

≡≡≡≡≡≡ ≡≡≡≡≡≡≡≡≡≡≡≡≡

Objection: Salvation indeed is merited by Christ perfectly, but it is not yet given. Answer: "And this is the record, that God hath given to us eternal life, and this life is in his Son. He that hath the Son hath life; and he that hath not the Son of God hath not life. These things have I written unto you that believe on the name of the Son of God; that ye may know that ye have eternal life, and that ye may believe on the name of the Son of God." {I Jn.5:11-13} Luther answers thus, "Christ hath saved us two ways already; first, he has perfectly done all things requisite to make us safe; and secondly, he hath bestowed all things already upon us, with himself; thirdly, faith in Scripture is termed a receiving; that is, a taking to a man's self, what is offered and delivered by another; as Joseph took unto himself Mary. Mt.1:24. So by faith we receive and possess righteousness, life and salvation, together with and in Christ."

=================================

Objection: Yet our knowledge and apprehension is weak and imperfect. Answer: 1. But we are known and apprehended by Christ perfectly, and that is full Salvation. 2. We are not justified fully in respect of our knowledge or faith, which is but in part, but objectively and completely in Christ our Surety. 3. The argument holds not from the quality to the Object. 4. Both Justification and Salvation be perfect in regard of God's Imputation and Donation, not of our apprehension. Imputation is perfect where faith is but little.

A. As this tenent was rather forced upon us, then caused by us to be made so public, so it is clear that we have the consent both of Scripture and approved authors, to warrant us so far as ever we held it, and consequently it appears how unjustly we are branded and condemned by you. B. A believer works freely and joyfully, having obtained already all salvation by free gift without works, through faith alone in Christ Jesus. C. And yet through hope he waits for the full revelation and sensible fruition, as well of the righteousness of faith, as of his adoption, redemption and Salvation by Christ; for our life is hid with God in Christ, &c. D. There is continual need of the faithful dispensation and diligent use of the word, ordinances, &c., that we may grow up in the knowledge of Christ, be established in the more full assurance of these exceeding and heavenly treasures to preserve our minds, that they be not corrupted, deceived, and carried away from the simplicity of faith in Christ Jesus.

The second proposition is that the Gospel and not the Law is the instrument of true sanctification. This was questioned by occasion of a sermon at St. Bartholomew's by the Exchange upon Galatians 4:22, where it was delivered that the Promise or the Gospel, and not the Law was the seed and doctrine of our new birth; yea, that the Law did not sanctify, &c., which divers ministers and others excepted against; and many affirmed that the Law was made effectual by Christ for that end and use, but their words wanted warrant and weight.

Neither doth it much move us, that they objected against the common practice, judgment and teaching of the ministry, since we are backed with a far more sacred and firm authority. For first, the holy Scripture doth sufficiently witness and justify our tenent. "Sanctify them through thy truth; thy word is truth." {Jn.17:17} Where observe, that to sanctify in the sense of the Hebrews, from whom this word is taken, is to separate anything from a profane and common use, and so to consecrate it to God, or to convert it to a sacred and divine use, and being here applied to a man it includes two things.

1. The justifying of him, by the communication of Christ's perfect holiness, whereby the believer is presented holy and without blame to God. Thus is sanctification taken also in Hebrews, "by the which will we are sanctified through the offering of the body of Jesus Christ once for all" – "for by one offering he hath perfected forever them that are sanctified;" {vs.10,14;} for so Zanchy expounds it, saying, "this perfect fulfilling of the will of God is the sanctification of Christ, and by this we are sanctified, because it is imputed to us."

2. An inward and sensible renewing or changing of the mind, by the operation of the Spirit of Christ, purifying the heart and life by degrees; of this latter branch or part is all the controversy, and yet what man of understanding, being well advised, would question it, seeing sanctification is inseparably annexed to Justification, as light is to the sun, and virtually is included in it, as the effect in the cause; or

naturally flows from it, as water from the fountain. Since the same Christ is the author of both, the same word of Truth reveals and communicates both, and faith is the instrument apprehending both. But if we note well what this word of truth is, it will be yet more evident, for this end compare these Scriptures: "In whom ye also trusted, after that ye heard the word of truth, the gospel of your salvation; in whom also after that ye believed, ye were sealed with that Holy Spirit of promise, which is the earnest of our inheritance until the redemption of the purchased possession, unto the praise of his glory." {Eph.1:13-14} "For the hope which is laid up for you in heaven, whereof ye heard before in the word of the truth of the gospel; which is come unto you, as it is in all the world; and bringeth forth fruit, as it doth also in you, since the day ye heard of it, and knew the grace of God in truth." {Col.1:5-6} So, it is plain that the word of Truth is no other word than the Gospel of our Salvation, and the antithesis used in John, "for the law was given by Moses, but grace and truth came by Jesus Christ;" {1:17,} shows that it is a peculiar and special prerogative of the Gospel to be called by that name, by way of excellency; the sense then is, that God doth sanctify his Church and people through faith, or by the hearing and believing of the Gospel.

"For the grace of God that bringeth salvation hath appeared to all men, teaching us that, denying ungodliness and worldly lusts, we should live soberly, righteously, and godly, in this present world." {Tit.2:11-12} Hence, I thus argue, what word teaches effectually to deny all ungodliness, and worldly lusts, and to live soberly, &c., that word sanctifies instrumentally, but the Gospel teaches so effectually; therefore, the assumption is plain thus, that the word in which that Grace that brings Salvation to God's elect doth appear, is none other but the Gospel;

and this word teaches men so, &c., therefore, it is the Gospel.

"But ye have not so learned Christ; if so be that ye have heard him, and have been taught by him, as the truth is in Jesus; that ye put off concerning the former conversation the old man, which is corrupt according to the deceitful lusts, and be renewed in the spirit of your mind." {Eph.4:20-23} That word is the instrument of sanctification in which Christ is taught and learned in truth, but that is the Gospel only that informs us concerning Christ, and acquaints us with Christ, &c.

"This only would I learn of you, received ye the Spirit by the works of the law, or by the hearing of faith?" {Gal.3:2} That word is the ordinary instrument of sanctification by which God conveys the Spirit of adoption and holiness, but that is by the Gospel and not by the Law, even by the hearing of faith; that is of the Gospel, the doctrine of faith, Rom.3:27, propounding justification and life freely without the works of the Law. To add further Scripture is to light a candle at noon day; if any yet please, let him read and consider carefully these passages: II Cor.3:18; I Jn.4:19; Rom.5:5; Gal.5:6; Jam.1:18; I Pet.1:21; Rom.15:16; Rom.8:2; Ezek.37:26, &c.

Also, however we are accused, we have walked directly in the steps of as sound and experienced divines as any are read or consulted with this day, but I will only record a few of their sentences as they came to my hand.

Augustine is full to this purpose. "The circumcision of the heart, to wit, a disposition to love Christ, cannot be effected by the Law or letter, teaching and threatening, but by the Spirit of the Gospel, prompting and moving the affections." Also, "what the Law of works commands in a threatening manner, that the Law of faith obtains by believing." Again, "in the Law of works God saith, do what I bid thee; in the Law of faith, it is said to God, Give, O Lord, what Thou commandest, and then command what Thou wilt." Again, "the Law is given that the Grace of the Gospel might be sought for; for Grace is given that the Law might be fulfilled; neither is it the fault of the Law that it is not fulfilled, but it is by the fault of the wisdom of the flesh, which fault is showed by the Law, but cured by the Grace of the Gospel."

Luther, on Galatians 3:2. "You have taught and heard the Law of Moses every Sabbath, but it was never yet perceived or seen that the Holy Ghost was given to any, either teacher or scholar, by the doctrine of the Law, &c., yea with great zeal and labor have you endeavored to express the Law by works, and so that you have been doers also of the Law, and yet you cannot show that ever this was done, but presently as soon as the hearing of faith or the Gospel came unto you, &c., by that only hearing of faith you received the Holy Spirit." Again, "the Holy Ghost hath never been given in the doctrine of the Law, neither can it be showed or proved by any example that it is ever so given. It necessarily therefore follows that the Holy Ghost is given by the preaching of Faith alone."

Perkins on that place, Gal.3:2, "here, saith he, we see the difference between the Law and the Gospel; the Law doth not minister the Spirit unto us, for it only shows our disease, and gives us no remedy; the Gospel ministers the Spirit, for it shows what we are to do, and for this purpose the Spirit is given, &c." And upon, Gal.2:19, "evangelical sorrow is sorrow for sin, because it is sin, and this indeed is a grace of God; but it is not wrought by the Law, but by the preaching of mercy and reconciliation, &c., the Law then being the cause of no good thing in us."

Cudworth on Gal.6:2, in regards to the last difference between the Law and Gospel hath these words, "the Law is no instrumental cause of faith, repentance, or any saving grace, &c., for this cause Paul calls the Law a dead or killing letter, and the Gospel a quickening spirit."

Calvin on John 6:29, "a notable place, saith he, that though men miserably weary themselves all their life, yet they lose their labor, except that faith in Christ be their rule of life; neither doth faith exclude either charity or any other good work since it contains all good works in it; for faith is called the only work of God, because possessing Christ by it, we are made the sons of God, that Christ might govern us by his Spirit; seeing Christ therefore doth not separate the fruit of it from faith, it is no surprise if he place all in it." On Romans 8:2, "the Law of Moses indeed is spiritual, commanding spiritual obedience, but it is not the Law of the Spirit, the instrument of the Spirit, nor the Ministry of life, but of death, &c."

Piscator on I Pet.1:5, "such as desire to be saved have need of the knowledge of the Truth; to wit, of that heavenly truth of which Christ praying for his disciples said, Jn.17:17, sanctify them with thy Truth, &c., and this is the word of the Gospel concerning Christ crucified for our Salvation."

Bullinger on Gal.4:1, "he that trusts in God through Christ is free from the Law, for he hath the Spirit of the Gospel henceforth to lead him, so that he needs not the Law; that is, the guidance and enforcement of the Law; neither can it condemn him with its curses, for such a one lives in Christ, and of himself, he is freely carried to the offices of piety; and so therefore it is said that the Law is not for the righteous, &c."

Tyndale in the Book of Obedience, saith, "he that is renewed in Christ keepeth the Law, without any Law written or compulsion of any ruler or officer, save by the Lord of that Spirit only." Also, "the spiritual do look Moses in open face, and are a Law to themselves, having a Law written in their hearts by the Spirit, and need not that any proffer them any reward for to keep the Law, for they do it naturally." Again, "heaven they take of the gift of God through Christ's deservings, and keep without all manner of doubt, that God according to his promise will defend them in this world, and do also for them of his goodness in Jesus Christ. Oh therefore love God and work freely."

Fox, in his Acts and Monuments, tells us that, "an error may be noted in the Papists touching the efficient or formal of good works, for albeit they all confess in their books that the grace of God is the chief and principal cause thereof, &c., yet all good works after regeneration they refer to other subordinate causes under God, as to free will, the habit of virtue or nature, and nothing at all to faith, when as faith alone under God is the root and fountain of all well doing, &c., so Paul, Mary, Zacchaeus the publican, and all the nations of the Gentiles began to bring forth fruit, and special good fruit, when they began to be engrafted into Christ." Again, "the office of faith is as to justify; and so the nature of it is to work by love, as the root by the sap. For as a man sees and feels by faith the love and grace of God towards him in Christ Jesus his Son; so begins he to love again both God and man, and to do to his neighbor, as God have done to him."

Lastly, Rollock, on John chapter 5, "what dost thou think faith else to be, than a feeling and tasting of the infinite mercy and love of God towards a man in Christ Jesus. This sense of that mercy and love of God towards us, is that which enlarges the heart, and melts the same into the mutual love of God, and into joy unspeakable; therefore above all things, I commend unto all faith in Christ, whilst I bid men believe, I bid them in so doing, to do all things; herein I bid them love God, I bid them to obey him in every kind; for all these flow from true faith."

It is objected, that the Law converts the soul. "The law of the LORD is perfect, converting the soul; the testimony of the LORD is sure, making wise the simple." {Ps.19:7} Answer: The Hebrew word Torah, used there and in divers other places, signifies any kind of doctrine; but these interpreters affirm that it is spoken of the doctrine of the Gospel, which is called the Law of faith. Rom.3:27. As also it is said the Law shall come out of Zion, "and many nations shall come, and say, Come, and let us go up to the mountain of the LORD, and to the house of the God of Jacob; and he will teach us of his ways, and we will walk in his paths; for the law shall go forth of Zion, and the word of the LORD from Jerusalem," {Mic.4:2;} that is, the Gospel which was to begin at Jerusalem, and so to be published and spread throughout the world.

But the Apostles in all their epistles exhort to work and walk according to the Law. Answer: True, and the Law in the matter of it is, so far as I know, never denied to be a rule, according to which a believer is to walk and live, and therefore I take the contrary allegation to being impudent slander. Yet secondly, the Law sanctifies not therefore, nor gives any heart or ability in truth to perform what it requires. Thirdly, but it calls upon a believer, and ministers occasion to him, for the expressing or showing forth of the same. If a father begets a merciful son, he bids him, as occasion is offered, to do a work of mercy, but not to make him pitiful, either by his bidding or his child's working, but to express his virtues in the relieving of the needy. "But ye are a chosen generation, a royal priesthood, an holy nation, a peculiar people; that ye should show forth the praises of him who hath called you out of darkness into his marvelous light." { I Pet.2:9}

═══════════════════════════════

Christian reader, here hast thou the very ground and tenent from which they conclude and condemn us for Antinomians, Enthusiasts, sons of Belial, Libertines, &c., is not this a goodly argument of theirs, that the Law sanctifies not, is not the seed of regeneration; nay, it hath no virtue or efficacy to renew or change the mind to produce any good fruit, &c., and therefore we destroy and abrogate the Law or deny the work and use of it. Indeed, the cause of their stumbling at our doctrine is the misinterpreting of that place, Rom.6:16, and others like unto it, not carefully observing the difference of our threefold estate of being; first without Law, in regard not of right, but of fact and practice; secondly, under the Law, where though we be convinced of the justice and equity of it, yet it can give no power to perform; and thirdly, under Grace, where alone we are made free indeed, &c., and the want of a distinct handling and applying of the Law and the Gospel to their proper end and uses.

  The Law hath its proper office and use as it revealeth sin, accuseth, terrifieth and condemneth; and we say with Paul that the Law is good, if a man use it lawfully; that is, if a man use it as a Law. If I define the Law rightly and keep it in its office and use, it is an excellent thing; but if I translate it to another use, and attribute what is not to be attributed to it; I not only then pervert the Law, but all Divinity. This discovereth the vanity of their profession; and saith, in whom Christ and the love of God in him doth not effectually move and constrain to walk worthy of so high and heavenly calling. Such have not heard Christ, nor been taught by Him, as the truth is in Jesus. True faith purifieth the heart, brings the soul into favor and communion with God, stayeth it upon his Name, causeth it to take delight in the multitude of heavenly peace, and so filleth and satisfieth it with that fullness and goodness of God, that it falleth off from all earthly and perishable felicity. "Love not the world, neither the things that are in the world. If any man love the world, the love of the Father is not in him." {I Jn.2:15} He that indeed finds this true treasure or pearl, sells everything and buys it, and lives joyfully and happily on it, as his portion or inheritance in the midst of the world's malice, contempt and worst entreaties.

Happy is he that could look into the clear fountain of goodness; Christ within would frame his mind better, than the Law could constrain by threatening and terrifying. Hereby that calumny is cleared, that if Christ free us from the subjection of the Law, it brings a liberty to sin. For Christ doth not send his children out to an unbridled wantonness, that without modesty they should revel as horses set loose in the fields, but he brings them to a course of living agreeable to the Law.

# **FINIS**

www.ingramcontent.com/pod-product-compliance
Lightning Source LLC
Chambersburg PA
CBHW070837100426
42813CB00003B/653